BATEMAN'S

East Sussex

Adam Nicolson

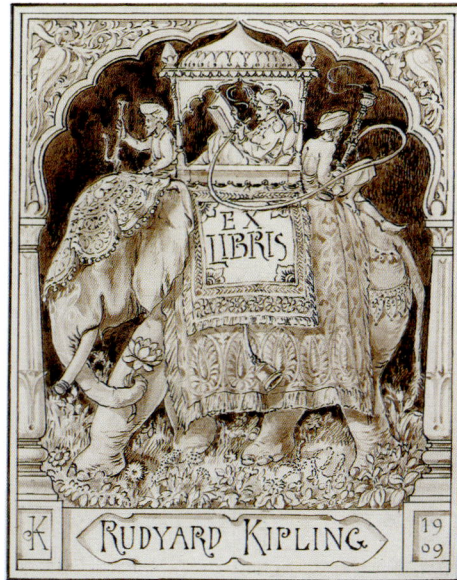

THE NATIONAL TRUST

CONTENTS

'A GOOD AND PEACEABLE PLACE'

'Behold us,' Rudyard Kipling wrote in November 1902, 'lawful owners of a grey stone lichened house – A.D.1634 over the door – beamed, panelled, with old oak staircase, and all untouched and unfaked. Heaven looked after it in the dissolute times of mid-Victorian restoration and caused the vicar to send his bailiff to live in it for 40 years and he lived in peaceful filth and left everything as he found it. It is a good and peaceable place standing in terraced lawns nigh to a walled garden of old red brick and two fat-headed oast-houses with red brick stomachs, and an aged silver-grey oak dovecot on top.'

Bateman's, looking now exactly as Kipling described it, was his idea of home, a sanctuary, private and protective, away from the noise of village and road, embedded in the richly wooded landscape of the Sussex Weald, 'a real House in which to settle down for keeps', as he described it in his auto-biography written at the end of his life. He and Carrie, his American wife, had found the house two years earlier but had been too slow in deciding to buy it, and Bateman's was let before they could close the deal. When the house came on the market again in the summer of 1902, they had no hesitation and bought it, the surrounding buildings including the mill, and 33 acres for £9,300. It had no bath-room, no running water upstairs and no electricity. 'We have loved it,' Kipling wrote at the time, 'ever since our first sight of it.'

He was 36 when he came to Bateman's, Carrie three years older. They had been married for ten years during which Kipling had become the most famous writer in the English-speaking world. His success was enormous. He was earning £5,000 a year by the end of the century, at a time when a secretary might have an annual salary of £80, and had been offered a knighthood, which he had

(Left) The south front

refused. Despite these outward triumphs, Kipling was in a fragile condition. Four perfect years in Vermont, where he had hoped they might live for ever, had been ruined eventually by a massively public row with Carrie's brother, Beatty. In 1899, their elder daughter Josephine, the girl for whom her father wrote the *Just So Stories*, had died aged six after a bout of pneumonia from which Kipling himself had suffered but recovered. 'His life was never the same after her death,' Elsie, his younger daughter, wrote later. 'A light had gone out that could never be rekindled.' Finally, the house where they had attempted to settle in Rottingdean was besieged by trippers and was anyway disturbing for its all-present memories of the dead girl. They needed a haven and an escape.

The calm and solid stability of Bateman's was the necessary balm. The house itself could be seen as an emanation of the soil, an English refuge which the Kiplings could dive into for privacy and quiet. It became an embodiment of the England they had come to rest in, of Sussex, of the Weald and more particularly of this small part of it, the Dudwell valley in which Bateman's sits. The walls, the mullioned windows, the pilasters and round arch of the porch which hint at the first tentative intrusions of the Renaissance into this obscure part of Sussex, are all built of a local sandstone. It is so local, in fact, that the quarry from which the house's stones were cut lies just across the lane from the garden gate opposite the front door. The tiles on the big hipped roofs and the bricks of the six-chimney stack that rises over the centre of the house are all baked from the clay of which the Weald is mostly composed. The internal structures, staircase and panelling are all cut from the oaks which grow so thickly here that they have been called the 'Sussex weed'. Bateman's clothed Kipling in the materials that were the foundations of his spiritual home.

CHAPTER ONE
TOUR OF THE HOUSE

The Approach

THE ORCHARD AND HERB GARDEN

The house is approached from the north by a path that skirts the orchard (the former kitchen garden), which is planted with old English varieties of fruit trees. The right-hand border is laid out as a herb garden, containing a large selection of herbs, both medicinal and culinary, such as Toadflax, Feverfew, Vervain, Sneezewort and Woad. Kipling put such atmospheric names to good use in his poem, 'Our Fathers of Old'. *Helichrysum italicum* has a curry scent redolent of India.

At the bottom of the slope is the Pear Alley, which was designed by Kipling and contains cordoned examples of 'Conference', 'Superfine' and 'Winter Nelis' pears, intertwined with clematis and underplanted with shade-loving species such as periwinkle and Corsican hellebore.

THE MULBERRY GARDEN

Leaving the tea-room on the right, you come to a wrought-iron gate incorporating Kipling's initials. This leads into the Mulberry Garden (the old wagon yard), where millstones punctuate the brick paths. The tree from which this garden took its name has gone, but was replaced in 1995 with a new black mulberry. The walls are covered with climbers, and the beds contain herbaceous plants and shrubs chosen for their hardiness (this is a frost hollow) and to provide year-long colour and interest: tree peonies, geraniums and shrub roses.

The opening scene from *A Doctor of Medicine*, one of Kipling's stories for his children collected in *Rewards and Fairies* (1910), is set here. His son John, then aged thirteen, and his daughter Elsie, a year older, appear as Dan and Una. The planting has changed in the intervening years:

They were playing hide-and-seek with bicycle lamps after tea. Dan had hung his lamp on the apple tree at the end of the hellebore bed in the walled garden, and was crouched by the gooseberry bushes ready to dash off when Una should spy him. He saw her lamp come into the garden and disappear as she hid it under her cloak. While he listened for her footsteps, somebody (they both thought it was Phillips the gardener) coughed in the corner of the herb-beds.

'All right,' Una shouted across the asparagus; 'we aren't hurting your old beds, Phippsey!'

Of course, it isn't the gardener coming, but Puck, the resident spirit and pagan deity who presides over the Dudwell valley and introduces the children to the history of England.

Beyond the Mulberry Garden, an arch in the yew hedge brings the visitor to the front of the house. A stone path runs between the front door and the garden gate. Here, as often as not, Kipling would greet a visitor. The prospect of meeting one of the most distinguished men of letters in the world could make visitors nervous and Kipling was expert at putting them at their ease. Here in June 1935, at the very end of Kipling's life, a young American journalist, Arthur Gordon, describes his reception:

When I found the sombre seventeenth century house and saw my host walking down to the gate to meet me, I grew so flustered that I hardly knew whether to shake hands or turn and run.

He was so small! The crown of the floppy hat he wore was not much higher than my shoulder, and I doubt if he weighed 120 pounds. His skin was dark for an Englishman's; his moustache was almost white. His eyebrows were as thick and tangled as marsh grass, but behind the gold-rimmed glasses his eyes were as bright as a terrier's. He was sixty-nine.

He saw instantly how ill at ease I was. 'Come in, come in,' he said companionably, opening the gate.

The entrance front

The House

The house was probably built in about 1634, the date over the porch. The only oddity about it is the asymmetry of the entrance front. It may well be that a gabled wing on the north side was planned to match the one that exists on the south but was never executed.

A large block of ironstone is incorporated into the porch, and a longstanding tradition claims Bateman's was built by a Wealden ironmaster. The first known occupant was a John Britten (or Brittan) at the end of the 17th century. He was an iron dealer rather than master and he may be the origin of the ironmaster story. Certainly Kipling believed it and treasured the many Sussex ironbacks and firedogs that furnish fireplaces throughout the house. It was an industry that used every aspect of the country. The fast-running streams drove the hammers and bellows of the forges. The iron was to be found in thick clots embedded in the local sandstone. The widespread sweet chestnut and hornbeam coppices, still covering much of the hill south of Bateman's, provided the wood from which the charcoal was made. On the gluey, impassable clay of the woodland tracks, the ironmasters threw down the spent clinker from their furnaces to make them usable in winter.

There were several forges in the valley of the Dudwell, both upstream and downstream of Bateman's, and it is plausible to think that one of the ironmasters lived here. For Kipling, a self-made man drawn as much to newness, enterprise and technology as he was to the stable continuities and stoicism of the agricultural life, this intimacy of Bateman's with Wealden iron added to its allure, an addition of flame and molten metal to the calming fields and 'the woods that know everything and tell nothing' of his chosen valley.

THE PORCH

Before entering the house, the visitor passes through the Porch. On its outer left-hand pier, carved into the sandstone, are the initials of the entire Kipling family: RK (Rudyard), CK (Carrie), EK (Elsie) and JK (John), as well as those of an unidentified friend, CM. Presumably cut by RK himself, it is the first sign at Bateman's of its owner's irrepressible sense of fun.

A pair of oak benches with backs made from 17th-century oak panelling.

RIGHT OF FRONT DOOR:

Beneath the light, referred to by Kipling as 'The Drunkard's Relief', is the *wrought-iron bell-pull* which once hung outside The Grange, the London home of the Pre-Raphaelite painter Edward Burne-Jones who married Kipling's aunt, Georgiana Macdonald. Kipling's childhood visits to The Grange, which he called 'the House of Enchantment', were the only oases of delight over five otherwise savagely unhappy years, alone with his little sister in the hands of a bullying landlady in Southsea. As he wrote in his autobiography, *Something of Myself*, the bell-pull became a sort of talisman for him, a guarantee of happiness in the house to which it gave access:

. . . arriving at the house, I would reach up to the openwork iron bell-pull on the wonderful gate that let me into all felicity. When I had a house of my own, and The Grange was emptied of meaning, I begged for and was given that bell-pull for my entrance, in the hope that other children might also feel happy when they rang it.

THE HALL

The 17th-century panelling, the simple stone doorways and the plain moulded fireplace of this room are all original, and were what first attracted Kipling to the house.

In 'They', a story about a father in search of his dead daughter, written soon after the Kiplings arrived at Bateman's and fuelled by his grief over the death of the six-year-old Josephine five years earlier, he describes his own hall, already resonant with loss:

I waited in a still, nut-brown hall, pleasant with late flowers and warmed with a delicious wood fire – a place of good influence and great peace. (Men and women may sometimes, after great effort, achieve a creditable lie; but the house, which is their temple, cannot say anything save the truth of those who have lived in it.) A child's cart and a doll lay on the black-and-white floor, where a rug had been kicked back. I felt that the children had only just hurried away – to hide themselves, most like – in the many turns of the great adzed staircase that climbed statelily out of the

The Hall

hall. . . . An old eagle-topped convex mirror gathered the picture into its mysterious heart, distorting afresh the distorted shadows . . .

At other times, more practical and urgent considerations overrode this melancholy and mysterious atmosphere. In the winter of 1911, as the children's governess remembered, the River Dudwell flooded and 'Mr Kipling on one occasion at least, dashed from his bed in the dead of night to rescue some valuable rugs from being submerged by the muddy water that welled over the great hall like a lake of pea-soup'.

Here too Kipling might meet his guests. The young novelist and playwright Rupert Croft-Cooke came to pay homage in 1922:

At 57, with his vast bushy eyebrows greying, his thick glasses and his bald pate, he attracted all my adolescent reverence towards a father figure, yet the little legs in plus-fours, the shortness, and something impish which instantly appeared, wiped out my awe and shyness, and I began to gabble of my journey.

FACING ENTRANCE DOOR:

The small window gave Mrs Kipling, whose office lay beyond it, a porthole through which she could survey anyone coming into the Hall.

Anxious to preserve his privacy and unhappy about talking to someone he could not see, Kipling refused to have a telephone at Bateman's. Urgent messages were sent by telegram or from the telephone in the village post office in Burwash.

The fireplace here was the greatest of all Kipling's allies in his attempts to protect his cherished privacy. Frank Doubleday, Kipling's American publisher, witnessed the following incident:

Kipling was crouched in front of a roaring fireplace, feeding the flames with bundles of papers. Even as the publisher stood in the doorway he saw a mass of manuscript in that well-known small handwriting go into the hearth. Every instinct of a publisher was appalled.

'For Heaven's sake, Rud,' he said 'what are you doing?'

Kipling, perspiring by the blaze, gave the mass of

9

burning papers a rummaging thrust with a poker. He looked at his friend keenly from under those heavy brows.

'Well, Effendi [A Turkish title of respect, punning on Doubleday's initials, F N D], I was looking over old papers and I got thinking. – No one's going to make a monkey out of me after I die.'

PICTURES

RIGHT OF ENTRANCE DOOR:

THOMAS MATTHEWS ROOKE (1842–1942)
The Dining Room at The Grange
Watercolour. Dated 1904
A Pre-Raphaelite interior. Kipling's uncle Burne-Jones rented The Grange in Fulham from 1867, and this view by his studio assistant shows it at his death in 1898. In the foreground is the table made as a wedding present for him by the architect Philip Webb in 1860. Burne-Jones himself decorated the

The Dining Room at The Grange; by T. M. Rooke, 1904 (Hall)

sideboard beyond at the same time (now in the Victoria & Albert Museum). The 'Sussex' chairs and the stained glass were made by Morris & Co. This is the 'paradise which I verily believe saved me', which Kipling visited for four Decembers from 1873 to 1876, the only times of happiness in the years of desolation. The picture had an almost sacred status for Kipling.

RIGHT OF FIREPLACE:

Sir EDWARD JOHN POYNTER (1836–1919)
Bateman's from the south-west
Watercolour. Signed with monogram and dated 1913
The row of pleached limes on the right had been planted by the previous owner in 1898, but the Kiplings created the rectangular pond, the yew hedges and paved paths. By Kipling's other painter uncle.

Sir EDWARD JOHN POYNTER (1836–1919)
The Quarterdeck
Watercolour. Signed with monogram and dated 1913
A view of the wide flagged terrace that was laid out to the south of the house at Bateman's.

INSIDE FRONT DOOR:

Sir EDWARD JOHN POYNTER (1836–1919)
The Grecian Temple
Watercolour. Signed and dated 1911

FURNITURE

A 17th-century Dutch oak draw-leaf table on massive legs carved with acanthus leaves and Ionic capitals.

AT EITHER END OF TABLE:

A pair of 18th-century armchairs modelled on an Italian Renaissance original.

Two 17th-century English oak benches.

TO RIGHT:

A 17th-century Indo-Portuguese oak cupboard with very finely carved linenfold panels. Probably brought from The Grange.

TO RIGHT:

An English brass lantern clock, made by Daniel Hoskins in London in the 1630s. It is a particularly fine and early example of this type of clock.

LEFT OF CUPBOARD:

An early 17th-century Italian walnut chair, with an embossed leather seat and back.

BEHIND CHAIR:

A fragment of a 16th-century Brussels tapestry.

BESIDE TAPESTRY:

An 18th-century Armada chest, made in Nuremberg. Iron chests such as this were fitted with elaborate locking mechanisms and were the forerunners of domestic safes. Despite their names, they have nothing to do with the Spanish Armada or the sea.

RIGHT OF WINDOW:

A late 18th-century oak corner cupboard, containing a collection of Indian brass candlesticks and vases.

METALWORK

A large Benares brass tray was a wedding present from Kipling's younger sister Trix in 1892. When his daughter Josephine was young, Kipling may have had tea with her on this tray.

ON INDO-PORTUGUESE CUPBOARD:

A Tibetan brass and copper jug and *a circular brass box* that Kipling christened 'the Priest's Collar Box'.

The fireback depicting the Annunciation was made in Sussex.

ABOVE FIREPLACE:

An Indian brass fish, once fitted with wheels, but so intensively played with by John and Elsie Kipling on this floor that the wheels fell off.

The door on the far side of the Hall leads to the Inner Hall.

THE INNER HALL

The robust, confidently carved oak staircase and most of the panelling is contemporary with the house. The marks of the adze are visible on both. Some of the upper panelling, lighter in tone and cut by a saw, was installed by the Kiplings on their arrival in 1902. The staircase, cut in green oak but now 'dark as teak', as Kipling described it, twisted as it dried and is visibly out of true.

SCULPTURE

ON WALLS:

Bronzed plaster reliefs depicting Mowgli and other characters from Kipling's early books, made by his father, John Lockwood Kipling. Kipling senior began his career as a ceramics designer in the Potteries, and went out to India to teach at an art school in Bombay, where Kipling was born in 1865. Kipling remained extraordinarily and lovingly close to his father right up until his death in 1911. About *Kim*, Kipling's masterpiece, for which many of the plaques here were intended as illustrations, the son later wrote:

I took it to be smoked over with my Father. Under our united tobaccos it grew like the Djin released from the brass bottle, and the more we explored its possibilities

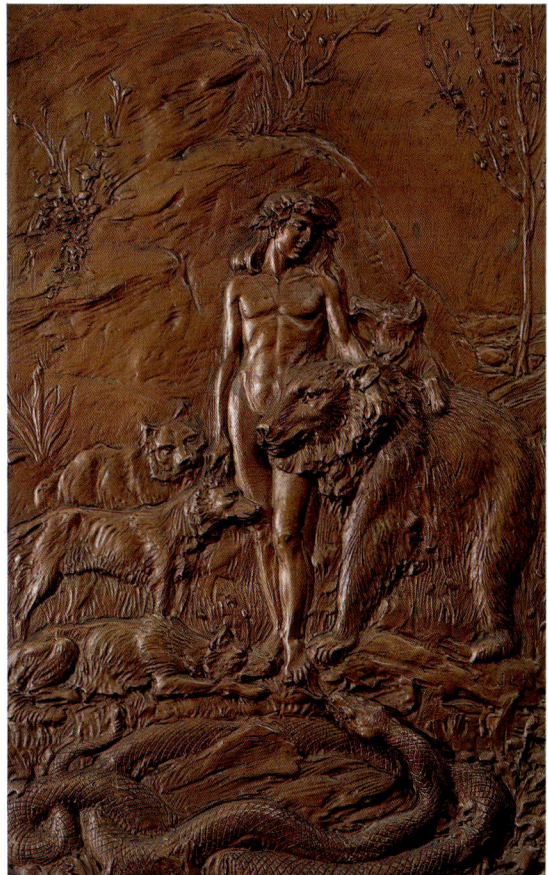

Mowgli; one of John Lockwood Kipling's bronzed plaster reliefs for 'The Jungle Book' (Inner Hall)

the more opulence of detail did we discover. I do not know what proportion of an iceberg is below waterline, but *Kim* as it finally appeared was about one-tenth of what the first lavish specification called for.

ON CORNER SHELF:

A gilt bronze and jewelled figure of the Buddha.

BELOW:

A terracotta of Ganesha, the Indian Elephant God.

PICTURE

A 17th-century map of Sussex.

FURNITURE

AT BOTTOM OF STAIRS:

A 17th-century English cupboard. It is almost certainly the top half of a taller piece. The turned bobbins in the upper part of the doors would have ventilated the inside, making it suitable for storing food.

TEXTILES

An English needlework sampler made by Mary Carman and dated 1779.

LIGHTING

A 17th-century brass chandelier, probably made in Holland. Larger versions of this model are often found in English village churches.

THE PARLOUR

Here, in front of the fire, Kipling would sit and talk to his guests. On his working mornings, the room was used by guests for their own reading or correspondence. In 1911 Stanley Baldwin, Kipling's cousin and later Conservative Prime Minister, was staying at Bateman's:

I am writing in the drawing-room, and Rud is upstairs, with his Muse in first-class working order, for I hear him tramping up and down and singing. Bless him! [A family term of endearment]

After dinner, it was the scene of games. One regular guest, Julia Catlin Taufflieb, describes the after-dinner rumpus:

Here Rud would play with his dogs. Down on the floor in front of the fire Rud would throw himself, and the dogs always knew it was their hour. The rugs were

turned up and a game of ball with Rud and his dogs was on the programme.

On other occasions, it was word games, at which of course Kipling excelled. Arthur Baldwin, Stanley's son, remembers one set of Consequences which Kipling began with the unforgettable ' "It's a perfect hell of a night," pouted the Duchess, unfastening her gaiters.'

It is in this room that the Kipling figure in his story 'They' finally encounters the touch of the dead child he is mourning and unconsciously seeking. The narrator is sitting listening to another's conversation about the cost of a shed, his hand quietly drumming on the Cordoba leather screen (see p.14):

I ceased to tap the leather – was, indeed, calculating the cost of the shed – when I felt my relaxed hand taken and turned softly between the soft hands of a child. So at last I had triumphed. In a moment I would turn and acquaint myself with those quick-footed wanderers . . .

The little brushing kiss fell in the centre of my palm – as a gift on which the fingers were, once, expected to close: as the all-faithful half-reproachful signal of a waiting child not used to neglect even when grown-ups were busiest – a fragment of the mute code devised very long ago.

It is the ghost of Josephine.

FURNITURE

'The worst of the place,' Kipling joked to a friend soon after arrival, 'is that it simply will not let us use modern furniture.' By the end of their lives, this Arts and Crafts austerity had sunk out of fashion (there had not even been a sofa in this room in the early days) and they had become famous for their 'uncomfortable hard-chaired home', as the novelist Hugh Walpole called it. Elsie Kipling came to dislike the way the house was furnished:

The stiff furniture is very much of the period of the house – about 1630 – with a resulting lack of comfort which my parents never seemed to notice. Many of the things were beautiful in themselves, but the whole effect was rather sparse and, in the winter, chilly.

IN MIDDLE OF ROOM:

A Knole sofa, one of many inspired by the 17th-century original at Knole, the great country house of the Sackvilles 25 miles to the north in Kent (also the property of the National Trust). It was re-covered in 1981, with a gift from the Beckenham & Bromley National Trust Centres.

The Parlour

LEFT OF DOOR:

An early 18th-century Dutch oak bombé (convex-shaped) bureau cabinet, used to display china (see below).

BEHIND SOFA:

A 17th-century Dutch oak table, which has lost the wide flat stretcher that would have joined the legs at floor level and balanced the rather top-heavy piece that we see today.

RIGHT OF CABINET:

An early 18th-century English games table.

UNDER WINDOW:

An early 17th-century French walnut refectory table. This, with the similar table in the Study (the room above), is one of the best pieces of furniture in the house. The subtlety of the turned columnar legs and the ingenious design on the base show how the Italian Renaissance had made its mark on France.

EITHER END OF TABLE:

Late 17th-century English walnut chairs, in a style that became popular during the reign of Charles II.

TO RIGHT:

A good mid-17th-century English oak cupboard. The top section is made up of a series of turned oak uprights with turned columns at the corners. It was used for storing food and is known as a 'dole cupboard', from dole, or bread, that was kept in similar cupboards and given out by the Church to the poor of the parish.

BETWEEN CUPBOARD AND FIREPLACE:

A fine English 17th-century side-table. It has lost the flap that would have echoed the shape of the top.

BESIDE FIREPLACE:

The log baskets were originally Dutch copper milk pails.

RIGHT OF FIREPLACE:

A 17th-century English oak table.

LEFT OF DOOR AS YOU LEAVE:

A screen made up from 18th-century embossed and painted 'Cordoba' leather that was left over once the Dining Room walls had been covered (see p.26).

An early 18th-century walnut-veneered cabinet, with a largely modern top.

'HOUSEHOLD GODS'

The cabinets both here and in Kipling's Study upstairs are full of tiny, privately assembled objects from the Far East and the distant past, Roman lamps, Greek harness, Indian, Chinese and Japanese figures and deities, a collection known to Kipling as his 'Household Gods'. Almost certainly blessed with psychic powers, as were his mother and sister Trix, Kipling was acutely aware of the role of the magical and the totemic in his life. These objects were more than assembled antiques for him.

CERAMICS AND OTHER ARTEFACTS

IN UPPER PART OF BUREAU CABINET:

Early 19th-century Chinese Nanking blue-and-white dishes.

ON CABINET:

An 18th-century faceted Dutch Delft vase, which is shown in the same position in a photograph taken of this room in 1908.

ON REFECTORY TABLE:

An English 18th-century mahogany cheese coaster, a Burmese silver bowl and a coloured gessoed box that was much treasured by Kipling. The last was a present from his daughter Elsie, who had bought it while on a visit to her fiancé, Captain George Bambridge, in Spain.

TEXTILES

On the floor are some of the fine oriental rugs that Kipling collected.

RIGHT OF DOOR:

A particularly fine Anatolian prayer rug.

UNDER WINDOW:

A long Samarkand prayer rug, made for children to pray on.

RIGHT OF WINDOW:

A fragment of 17th-century Flemish tapestry.

PICTURES

FLANKING BUREAU:

After GERARD DOU (1613–75)
Woman with candle and lantern
Dou was a pupil of Rembrandt who specialised in small and immaculately painted interiors.

J. M. CULVERHOUSE
Signed and dated [18]57
Woman with a candle

Two framed collections of Chinese watercolours painted on rice paper.

FLANKING FIREPLACE:

Sir AMBROSE POYNTER (1867–1923)
Rottingdean from the churchyard
Dated 1887
A view of the Sussex village where Kipling lived from 1897 until he moved to Bateman's in 1902. Poynter was Kipling's cousin and best man at his wedding in 1892. He was also an architect, directing the improvements to the main house and converting the oast-houses at Bateman's for the Kiplings' servants.

ANONYMOUS
Lake Rudyard
Watercolour
The lake in Staffordshire where Kipling's parents first met, in 1863, and after which he was named.

LIGHTING

RIGHT OF BUREAU CABINET:

A Tiffany Studio lamp. The American Art Nouveau designer Louis Comfort Tiffany set up his firm of interior decorators in New York in 1878. The bronze base has been artificially patinated and supports a shade made from coloured glass, which is held in place by a bronze framework. Another Tiffany lamp stands to the right of the fireplace. Carrie Kipling was American, and the couple spent their early married life, from 1892 to 1896, in the United States.

THE STAIRCASE

Arthur Baldwin describes a moment on the staircase, as his father Stanley, the Prime Minister, and his cousin Rudyard, the first English winner of the Nobel Prize for literature, enjoy a joke:

The Staircase

Another time, . . . these two middle-aged men were discovered sitting on the stairs, their arms round one another's shoulders, rocking and weeping with ungovernable mirth. What the cause of it was neither would ever say. I can promise you it wasn't liquor, anyway.

TEXTILES

The 17th-century Brussels tapestry depicts the enthroned Queen of Sheba surrounded by her attendants.

A needlework map of England and Wales, worked by Eliza Mullinex in 1796, when she was nine years old.

PICTURES

ON HALF-LANDING:

JOHN COLLIER (1850–1934)
Rudyard Kipling (1865–1936)
Signed and dated 1900
Painted while Kipling was living at The Elms, Rottingdean, and working on the final stages of *Kim*.

ON TOP LANDING:

WILLIAM NICHOLSON (1872–1949)
Rudyard Kipling (1865–1936)
Hand-coloured woodcut
Made in the summer of 1897 at the Burne-Joneses' Sussex home in Rottingdean for the *New Review* and later included in Nicholson's *Twelve Portraits* (1899). Nicholson and Kipling became friends, taking long walks together on the Downs. Kipling provided verses for Nicholson's *Almanac of Twelve Sports* (1897). The low viewpoint subtly disguises Kipling's shortness (he was 5ft 6in).

'SPY' (SIR LESLIE WARD) (1851–1922)
Rudyard Kipling (1865–1936)
Typical of the cartoons of the famous which 'Spy' produced for *Vanity Fair* between 1873 and 1909.

ANDRÉ CASTAIGNE (active 1885–1911)
'*Remember that you have sat with the Emperor of Britain and Gaul*'
Painted in 1906. The title is a quotation from *Puck of Pook's Hill* (1906), and the painting one of a series of illustrations done for the book. Kipling had admired the picture when on exhibition and it was later presented to him by the artist as 'a humble token of my admiration for your genius' (see framed letter below).

FURNITURE

IN FAR CORNER:

A longcase clock, with rocking-ship movement, made by Jonathan Williams of Bideford in the late 18th century.

OPPOSITE:

A late 19th-century copy of a mid-17th-century oak cupboard, carved in Gothic style with a figure of the Virgin and linenfold panels.

The door on the right as you reach the top of the Staircase leads to the Study.

THE STUDY

This was Kipling's work room. It is the heart of Bateman's and remains almost exactly as he left it. His routine was described by his daughter:

R.K. usually worked in the morning, if he had anything in hand, either doing the actual writing, or pacing up and down his study humming to himself. Much of his best known verse was written to a tune. . . . If he was really busy with a piece of work he was utterly absorbed in it and quite oblivious to anything else. Thus his children learned very early to keep any requests or plans until he was safely finished whatever was engaging him, until he 'came back' as they called it, and was again ready to enter their daily life.

Almost always, writing here was a solitary event, but it seems that Kipling liked to flatter occasional friends by admitting them to his Study while he was writing. Rider Haggard described one such occasion in September 1911:

On Sunday and Monday I sat in the study while [Kipling] worked and after a while he got up and remarked to me that it was odd but that my presence did not bother him a bit – he supposed because we were two of a trade but that when the other day some friend of his, Jameson or another – I forget who, had been in the room with him it had upset him altogether. With me present he could work as well as though he were alone.

But then, in the afternoons, with no writing to be done, as Julia Taufflieb describes:

After tea Rud would say, 'Well Julia, how about a story?' and we would go up to the study and he would light the fire. I stretched out on the settle and in truth it could never have been any other piece of furniture, so hard was it. But what did I care! Rud would take up one of his manuscripts, and read aloud one of his latest stories. He read delightfully, and lost himself completely in his reading. When he came to some pathetic passage he would 'choke up' and when there was a funny part, how he would laugh!

Years before, he had written to the American novelist E.L. White: 'I wonder if people get a tithe of the fun out of my tales than [*sic*] I get in doing 'em.'

FURNITURE

IN FRONT OF WINDOW:

The large early 17th-century French walnut draw-leaf table is the desk at which Kipling wrote. He describes it in his autobiography:

I always kept certain gadgets on my work table, which was ten feet long from North to South and badly congested. One was a long, lacquer, canoe-shaped pen-tray full of brushes and dead 'fountains'; a wooden box held clips and bands; another, a tin one, pins; yet another, a bottle slider, kept all manner of unneeded essentials from emery-paper to small screw-drivers; a

Kipling at his desk in the Study

paperweight, said to have been Warren Hastings', a tiny, weighted fur-seal and a leather crocodile sat on some of the papers; an inky foot-rule and a Father of Penwipers which a much loved housemaid of ours presented yearly, made up the main-guard of these little fetishes. . . . Left and right of the table were two big globes, on one of which a great airman had once outlined in white paint those air-routes to the East and Australia which were well in use before my death.

Kipling also mentioned 'an outsize office pewter inkpot, on which I would gouge the names of the tales and books I wrote out of it'. Apart from the leather crocodile, which was given to a naval friend, and the 'Father of Penwipers', the table remains virtually unchanged.

Kipling wrote on large pale blue pads specially made for him. On the blotter is a facsimile of the Charter of the River, a mock-medieval document drawn up by Kipling on 19 June 1906 which assigned to his children the 'Liberties, Freedoms & Benefits all and singular of that portion of the Dudwell River lying and situate between Turbine Point and the Great Ash commonly called Cape

Turnagain for their private and particular use, behoof, advantage, ownership, disport and delight' (illustrated on p.43).

Kipling left an extraordinarily exact account of his working practice, a habit of omission and elision which gives his later stories their air of density, rigour and surprise:

Take of well-ground Indian Ink as much as suffices and a camel-hair brush proportionate to the inter-spaces of your lines. In an auspicious hour, read your final draft and consider faithfully every paragraph, sentence and word, blacking out where requisite. Let it lie by to drain as long as possible. . . .

I have had tales by me for three or five years which shortened themselves almost yearly. The magic lies in the Brush and the Ink. For the Pen, when it is writing, can only scratch; and bottled ink is not to compare with the ground Chinese stick.

This way of working has left its marks, quite literally, on the table. In the Inventory, made in 1939 on Carrie's death, the valuer's only remark about this beautiful desk is: 'Black ink stains.'

Kipling was, in fact, extraordinarily messy and the ordered calm of the room as you now see it would not have been its condition when Kipling

The Study

was at work here. He, like the table, would probably have been covered in ink. When a young man
in India, he had received frequent dressing downs
for his appearance, his suit usually spotted with
ink-stains 'like a Dalmatian dog'.

BESIDE DESK:

The large Algerian waste-paper basket was much used:
'Mercifully, the mere act of writing was, and always
has been, a physical pleasure to me. This made it
easier to throw away anything that did not turn out

well: and to practise, as it were, scales.' Work would
often go through four or five drafts and at times the
desk was a chaos. In 1920 Kipling wrote in late
apology to Rider Haggard, one of his oldest and
closest friends, thanking him for his most recent
book: 'Like a fool I wrote you my thanks for "Smith
& the Pharaohs" and posted it under a blotter on my
dunghill of a table! Well, *you* know what my table is
like so I won't even attempt to apologize.'

On another occasion an entire chapter of Kipling's book on the Irish Guards in the Great War
disappeared. The secretary was accused of mislay-
ing it and for a week or two Kipling walked about

humming, as he did when irritated, until the type-script turned up, having been pushed by Kipling into another book in the Study.

ON DESK:

A 'Good Companion' Imperial typewriter. Kipling's secretary did most of his typing, after she had finished with Carrie's correspondence. Kipling himself used it only occasionally, as he was a poor typist: 'The beastly thing simply *won't* spell', he complained.

Two onyx ashtrays decorated with terriers. Kipling owned a string of Aberdeen terriers in later life, called Jimmy, Mike and Wampho.

A *wooden box* decorated in gesso with oak and ash leaves, and inscribed 'England shall bide till judge-ment tide in oak and ash and thorn', a quotation from *Puck of Pook's Hill*. It had been made by Johair Singh in 1879 in the Lahore Museum, of which Lockwood Kipling was curator, and 30 years later was inscribed and given to Kipling by his father.

IN FRONT OF TABLE:

An early 18th-century English walnut armchair, which was raised on blocks to make it exactly the right height for the table.

BELOW SMALL WINDOW:

An elaborately painted Indian red lacquer bridal chest.

BY DOOR:

A mid-17th-century English oak coffer. It has a par-ticularly well-carved front panel that, by its curved fluting, attempts to introduce a third dimension.

BEYOND:

A late 19th-century copy of a mid-17th-century oak cupboard, a pair to the one on the landing.

ON SIDE-TABLE:

A model frigate, Liverpool-rigged and made in the first half of the 18th century.

RIGHT OF FIREPLACE:

An oak day-bed, made at the beginning of this century. According to Elsie Kipling:

Lying on his side, his head propped on his right hand, my father spent many hours on this sofa while he brooded over the work he was busy with at the moment. From time to time he would jump up and go to the desk, write a line or two, make a note or correction, then resume his place on the sofa.

The day-bed was an essential part of the writing process. He explained its purpose to a young American, Arthur Gordon, in 1935:

'I lie there,' he said with a smile, 'and wait for my daemon to tell me what to do.'
  'Daemon?'
  He shrugged. 'Intuition. Subconscious. Whatever you want to call it.'

The Indian red lacquer bridal chest in the Study

'Can you always hear him?'

'No,' he said slowly. 'Not always. But I learned long ago that it's best to wait until you do. When your daemon says nothing, he usually means no.'

Before his doctors advised him to take up a pipe, Kipling smoked 30 to 40 cigarettes a day, a good proportion of them lying here. We should imagine the room blue with smoke. The valuer in 1939 provides a footnote to half a lifetime's thinking: 'Ledge of settee: cigarette burned.'

BOOKS

Two walls are lined with books. This was Kipling's working library; he did not look after it:

My treatment of books, which I looked upon as tools of my trade, was popularly regarded as barbarian. Yet I economised on my multitudinous pen-knives, and it did no harm to my fore-finger. There were books which I respected, because they were put in locked cases. The others, all the house over, took their chances.

The contents of the library reflect the man, not only the classics of English literature and perhaps 500 volumes on India (about a quarter of the total), large sections on the Navy and the Empire, but 21 separate books on bees and beekeeping, 20 on angling, 28 on Freemasonry (he had become a Mason in Lahore in 1885). Kipling came to Bateman's to learn about England, and the shelves, particularly at the far end of the room to the left of the window, are full of the rural England he was so greedily drinking in. Not only a *History of Sussex* so used that its binding is battered and loosened, a *Dictionary of the Sussex Dialect*, annotated and ink-blotted, but a complete set of Richard Jefferies, two or three volumes of W. H. Hudson, as well as *Practical Poultry Keeper, Talks on Manures, The Complete Grazier, Fences, Gates and Bridges* and H. C. Barkley's *Studies in the Art of Rat-Catching* (1911).

PICTURES AND SCULPTURE

ABOVE FIREPLACE:

PHILIP BURNE-JONES (1861–1926)
Caroline Kipling (1862–1939)
Inscribed 'P. B-J to R. C. K' and dated 1899
Caroline Balestier married Kipling in 1892. The key that hangs from her waist symbolises her role as mistress of the house. At Bateman's, she ran both the house and the estate, towards the end opening all incoming letters and signing all the cheques. She fiercely protected Kipling from the consequences of his fame. Painted by Kipling's cousin.

ABOVE CENTRAL SECTION OF BOOKCASE
ON LEFT:

The original sepia watercolour design for Kipling's bookplate, drawn by his father.

TO LEFT:

A terracotta low-relief self-portrait by John Lockwood Kipling, inscribed *Fumus Gloria Mundi* ('Smoke – the Glory of the World'). Kipling inherited his father's addiction to tobacco.

ON EITHER SIDE:

A Walker & Cockerell photograph of a painting of Burne-Jones at work, by his son Philip.

A photographic portrait of Dr L. Storr Jameson, leader of the abortive 'Jameson's Raid' against the Boer government of the Transvaal in South Africa in 1895. Jameson was one of Kipling's heroes and inspired his most famous poem, 'If'. He visited Bateman's in 1909.

Photograph of Josephine Kipling in gilt embossed circular frame.

BESIDE SMALL WINDOW:

Photograph of the launching of HMS Kipling, which was performed by Elsie Bambridge in 1939. During the fall of Crete in 1941, the *Kipling* picked up survivors from the sinking of the *Kelly,* and although herself badly damaged, brought them safely back 400 miles to Alexandria.

TEXTILES

A set of four Indian rugs, woven for Kipling at the beginning of the century.

THE WEST BEDROOM

This small spare bedroom was used by such distinguished visitors as Rider Haggard, who slept in 'an old Elizabethan bed' which, he had been told by the Kiplings, 'had always been in the house'.

Of the others who stayed here, Stanley Baldwin in particular was a ferocious walker, storming off on 20-mile route marches through the Sussex landscape. One day, after the Great War, he returned to

Rudyard Kipling; by John Collier, 1891 (West Bedroom)

Painted wearing an Indian tunic during the period when he was living in London and achieved rapid literary success.

JAMES McNEILL WHISTLER (1834–1903)
Old Battersea Bridge and *Old Westminster Bridge*, 1859
Etchings
The Forge and *Shop Front*
Lithographs
Whistler and Kipling are linked by a mutual friend, the American journalist Wolcott Balestier, whose sister was to marry Kipling.

FURNITURE

Except for the bed, the furniture is nearly all oak, English and 17th-century.

CERAMICS

Pearlware jug, decorated by John Lockwood Kipling, with the figures of Bacchus, god of wine, and a male accompanist, for his brother-in-law, the Rev. Frederick Macdonald.

his room to find the following notice pinned up on the wall:

RULES FOR GUESTS
1. No guest to walk more than 5 miles an hour.
2. No guest to walk more than two hours at a time.
3. Guests are strictly forbidden to coerce or cajole the natives to accompany them in said walks, as the proprietors cannot be responsible for the consequences.
Signed Rudyard Kipling
Caroline Kipling
Elsie Kipling (natives)

At the end of the First World War and afterwards, as Kipling was preparing *The Irish Guards in the Great War*, many officers came to stay, usually spending the night in this room.

PICTURES

The Crucifixion with Saints
Arundel Society chromolithograph, dated 1872, of a triptych by Pietro Perugino (1445–1523)

JOHN COLLIER (1850–1934)
Rudyard Kipling
Signed and dated 1891

THE EXHIBITION ROOM

The large room next to the Study was once a bedroom. The modern panelling was put in by the Kiplings, using oak from the Bateman's estate. It now houses an exhibition put together with the help of Elsie Kipling, with the intention of illustrating, through facsimiles of documents and other objects, his life and work.

IN FIREPLACE:

A very important fireback, the original of which is dated 1636. It depicts a Sussex ironmaster standing with his dog and surrounded by the tools and products of his trade. For centuries iron-making was an important industry in this part of Sussex, as Kipling recalled in 'Puck's Song':

Out of the Weald, the secret Weald,
Men sent in ancient years
The horse-shoes red at Flodden Field,
The arrows at Poitiers!

IN FRONT OF FIREPLACE:

A wrought-iron pipe kiln. It was used to clean the long clay pipes that were kept at inns for the use of travellers. When the pipes had become foul from tobacco juice, they were gathered together and sent

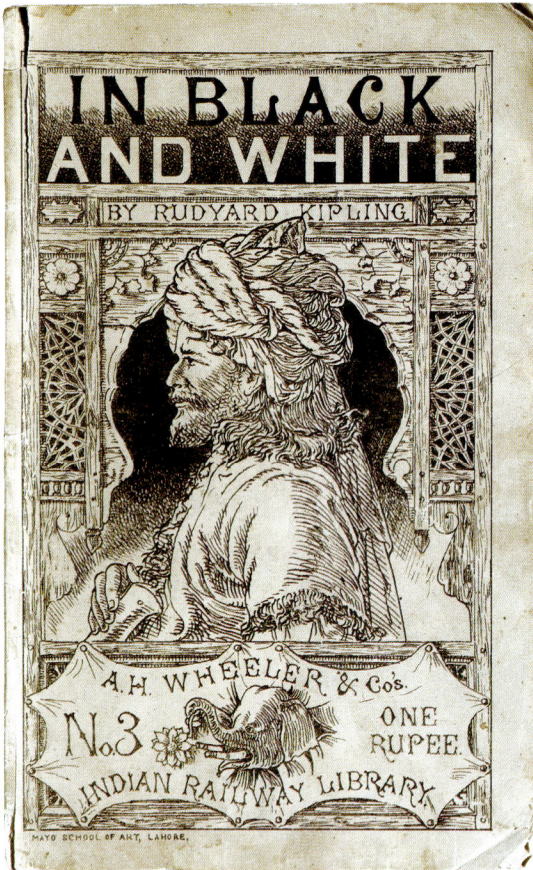

The cover for 'In Black and White', which was published in Allahabad in 1888 and contained eight of Kipling's early Indian short stories (Exhibition Room)

in a pipe kiln to the local baker, who would put them into a very hot oven, and bake them till clean.

RIGHT OF FIREPLACE:

A walnut armchair, designed by Sir Herbert Baker, the architect of the Woolsack, a house on the South African estate of Cecil Rhodes which was given to Kipling on a life tenancy, and where he and his family wintered from 1900 until 1908. The lower rail of the back is carved with the date 1924, the year in which Elsie married Captain George Bambridge, and the initials 'B K' (Bambridge Kipling).

Two 17th-century oak tables.

ON TABLE:

The Nobel Prize for Literature, awarded to Kipling in 1907. He spent the prize money on the garden at Bateman's. Many honours were offered to Kipling, but he accepted only literary and academic ones.

The Bateman's Visitors' Book, which was written up by Kipling after each visitor had departed. The entries run from 15 September 1902 to 6 January 1936, twelve days before Kipling's death.

PICTURES

The walls are hung with portraits of Kipling, and a series of plaster and terracotta plaques made by his father, depicting scenes from his early books.

After PHILIP BURNE-JONES (1861–1926)
Rudyard Kipling (1865–1936)
Kipling working at his desk at The Elms, Rottingdean, in 1899. The pewter inkpot still sits on his desk in the Study at Bateman's. Photogravure published in 1900. The original painting is in the National Portrait Gallery, London.

WILLIAM STRANG (1859–1921)
Rudyard Kipling (1865–1936)
Etching. Dated 1898

M. FULLER
The oast-houses at Bateman's
Watercolour. Dated 1895

ANONYMOUS
Park Mill
Painted in 1907
Kipling converted the mill to provide electricity for the house (see p.31). The converted oast-house on the left was occupied by Dorothy Ponton, first John and Elsie's governess, and then Kipling's secretary.

THE POWDER CLOSET

Wigs became fashionable for men in Britain from the 1660s, and small ante-rooms of this kind were occasionally set aside for the messy business of powdering them.

PICTURES

A series of coloured lithographs by the twin brothers E.J. and C.M. Detmold, commissioned for Kipling's first *Jungle Book*. The original watercolours were painted in 1902. One, of *Kaa the Python*, by C.M. Detmold, is exhibited here.

Kaa the Python;
watercolour by
C. M. Detmold,
1902 (Powder Closet)

THE KIPLINGS' BEDROOM

As one might expect of people who guarded their privacy as closely as the Kiplings, the life of the bedroom is quite unknown. No servant has left any record of what they knew, no friend or acquaintance was ever admitted. A limerick written by Kipling in 1911, when Elsie was fifteen, describes, charmingly and jokingly, the culture of privacy and mutual protectiveness which both Kipling and Carrie fostered:

There was a young person of Bateman's
Who was guarded in most of her statements.
　　When they asked 'Where's your pa?'
　　She said – 'Out in his car',
Whereas he was really in Bateman's.

More fiercely and more urgently to an American reporter in 1896, Kipling had made this impromptu speech, what amounts to a testament of his belief in his own life as his personal property:

I decline to be interviewed. American reviewing is brutal and immoral. It is an outrage to be insulted on the public highways and asked to give the details of one's private life. . . . Your copyright laws have swindled me out of considerable money. Is it not enough to steal my books without intruding on my private life? When I have anything to say, I write it down and sell it. My brains are my own.

All that can be said is that here, in this most private of rooms, the Kiplings gathered their memories of their three children. In a sense, it takes on the air of a shrine to nurtured grief. Each death in turn destroyed something in their father. Frank Doubleday had the task in 1899 of telling Kipling that Josephine had died. Kipling was still in his own sick bed: 'I took a seat beside him and told the story in as few words as I could. He listened in silence till I had finished, then turned his face to the wall.' Sixteen years later, another American, Julia Taufflieb, saw the Kiplings three months after John had been reported missing while serving on the Western Front:

I was in London in December 1915, and went to see the Kiplings at Brown's Hotel. One could never imagine that a tragedy had occurred in their lives. They seemed absolutely cheery and evidently had not allowed themselves to believe they would not see John again. However Rud, seeing me to my car that evening, at the foot of the stairs, took hold of my arm, and pressing it so that it almost hurt, said, 'Down on your knees, Julia, and thank God that you have not a son.' I knew then that he knew. Rud was never the same in any shape or manner after John's death.

Elsie, as the only survivor, carried much of the burden of her grieving parents. After they too had died, she wrote:

23

The Kiplings'
Bedroom

The two great sorrows of their lives, my parents bore bravely and silently, perhaps too silently for their own good. My mother hardly ever spoke of her two lost children, but sometimes my father would talk of them to me. There is no doubt that little Josephine had been his greatest joy during her short life. He always adored children, and she was endowed with a charm and personality (as well as enchanting prettiness) that those who knew her still remember.

BED

The oak four-poster bed is late 19th-century. The crewelwork bedspread and curtains, which incorporate the Kiplings' initials, are an exact copy of those on the bed in Kipling's time, whose style, technique and motifs were inspired by 17th-century embroidery. They were copied by the East Sussex Embroiderers Guild, because, unfortunately, the originals had faded almost to nothing and had become too delicate to leave on show. Textiles are very susceptible to light damage, and the National Trust uses blinds in its houses to prevent this.

OTHER FURNITURE

A late 17th-century English walnut day-bed.

A late 17th-century oak chest-of-drawers.

An 18th-century English oak wardrobe.

IN FRONT OF WINDOW:

An early 18th-century English oak lowboy on cabriole legs.

A stool on similar legs, the seat of which is upholstered in tapestry with laurel wreaths worked by Mrs Kipling.

TEXTILES

The window curtains are modern replacements, bought in 1985.

A needlework map of England by Elizabeth Ingram.

PICTURES

The portraits of Kipling's children include a pastel painted by E. Holbrook in New York of Josephine.

The three small caricatures framed together are also of Kipling's children, by their great-uncle, Burne-Jones. They were drawn at The Grange over Christmas 1897.

SCULPTURE

HENRY PEGRAM (1862–1937)
Elsie Kipling (1896–1976)
Signed and dated 1907. Circular bronze relief in oak frame
Kipling's younger daughter, who gave Wimpole Hall in Cambridgeshire to the National Trust.

THE DINING ROOM

Lunch at Bateman's was at one o'clock, dinner at eight. A hatch between the Dining Room and Kitchen was one of the first changes made at Bateman's.

The Kiplings always changed for dinner, even when alone. Kipling had enjoyed highly spiced food from his time in India and liked reading old cookery books, but in later life he was afflicted with duodenal ulcers, which obliged him to adopt a plainer diet: steamed fish, chicken and junket was a typical menu. Perhaps for this reason, visitors often found the food at Bateman's boring, although the wine was good. Kipling himself generally preferred cider, drunk from a pewter tankard. If there were people to tea, as was often the case, they would have it here or on the Hall table. There was always quite a lot to eat. Thin bread and butter, with medlar jelly or blackberry jam, hot buttered scones and 'piles of home-made cakes' was the usual pattern.

The relaxed atmosphere could lead the young and nervous into indiscretion. This is the eighteen-year-old Rupert Croft-Cooke, who had just published a book of verses about Sussex, having a Bateman's tea in 1922:

Mrs Kipling seemed to me that day a gentle motherly person, with dignity but without condescension, who put me – too much, I fear – at my ease and encouraged me to chatter.

She sat at the head of the table, Kipling was on her right and I on her left, and when their daughter arrived,

The Dining Room

cheerful, hungry and in tweeds, she sat beside me.

'Victor Neuberg [an eccentric author and publisher] says you're a minor poet, sir, who has written one major poem,' I piped across the table.

It was Mrs Kipling who asked, smiling, which poem that was.

'"The Mary Gloster"', I said triumphantly, but no one was to be drawn.

The more reverential literary pilgrims Kipling would shock or tease out of their stiffness, making his Aberdeen terriers run round the room taking a biscuit from the seat of every chair as they passed or, as the sanctimonious guests buttered their scones, repeating to them the story that during the war the Germans made margarine out of their soldiers' corpses, followed by this electrifying quatrain:

Charlotte, when she saw what Hermann
Yielded up when he was dead,
Like a well-conducted German
Spread him thickly on her bread.

It was not the Kipling his public reputation might have prepared them for.

WALL-HANGINGS

The early 18th-century English 'Cordoba' leather hangings take their name from Cordoba in Spain, where their manufacture originated in the 9th century. The sections are made up of panels of calfskin joined together invisibly. They are covered with a silver foil, followed by a yellow varnish to simulate gold. When this was dry, the surface was stamped or tooled, after which the design, borrowed from Chinese wallpaper, was applied in oil paint.

Carrie's diary for 9 August 1902 contains a brief note: 'To I of Wight to buy stamped Venetian leather for Bateman's'. By 23 August Rudyard is writing to Ambrose Poynter, his cousin and architect, to say, 'The leather has been bought and is now in our possession. It is lovelier than our wildest dreams and will need immense care.' Elsie remembered them bringing it to the house in their car, sticking out of the back like rolls of lino.

FURNITURE

The near-matching set of 18th-century mahogany Chippendale chairs has tapestry seat covers worked by the Royal School of Needlework with a design inspired by the hangings.

A 17th-century Flemish oak draw-leaf table.

A 17th-century English oak court cupboard, the upper doors of which have deeply recessed panels inlaid with holly and ebonised teak.

OPPOSITE COURT CUPBOARD:

A 17th-century French coffer. The design of the carved panels that make up the front is of Gothic origin and shows how long-lived this medieval style of decoration was in France.

The fire-screen is made of a piece of antique Indian embroidery depicting scenes from the life of the Hindu god Krishna. Embroideries of this kind are used as a ceremonial covering for trays of gifts at Hindu weddings.

PICTURES

OVER FIREPLACE:

After GUIDO RENI (1575–1642)
Virgin and Child
Carrie often sat at table with her back to this painting, which both Kiplings disliked, but were unable to remove, because it was a present. Kipling sat opposite her, but was so short-sighted that the picture did not bother him.

MS illumination of Christ and his Disciples in a 16th-century Italian carved gilt-wood frame.

CERAMICS AND METALWORK

The fireplace contains a Pither stove and is lined with Dutch earthenware tiles.

An illuminated miniature of Christ and his Disciples hangs on the 18th-century English 'Cordoba' leather in the Dining Room

ON COURT CUPBOARD:

A French Nevers faience apothecary's bowl. Faience is the French equivalent of Dutch Delft pottery.

A pair of late 18th- or early 19th-century Kashmir copper ewers, in 'Bokharah' style.

LIGHTING

The lampshades are made of panels of abalone shell, c.1918.

Visitors pass through the Hall again (described on p.8) to reach Elsie Kipling's Sitting Room.

ELSIE KIPLING'S SITTING ROOM

When the Kipling family first came to Bateman's, this room, which is lined with 17th-century panelling, became the Schoolroom, where the two children, Elsie and John, had their lessons under the direction of a governess. In 1912, when Elsie was sixteen, it was made into a sitting-room for her, and this use is echoed in its present arrangement. She was devoted to her father, living at Bateman's until her marriage in 1924, and returning frequently in his later years.

In its previous incarnation as a schoolroom, this is the setting of a tiny, remembered scene in 'A Centurion of the Thirtieth', one of the stories in *Puck of Pook's Hill.* Dan, the name given to John Kipling, is late coming up into the wood to meet Parnesius, the Roman Centurion, because, in a typical Kipling, teasing touch, he 'had come to grief over his Latin'. Eventually, Puck brings him up:

'We should have come sooner,' Puck called, 'but the beauties of your native tongue, O Parnesius, have enthralled this young citizen.'

Parnesius looked bewildered, even when Una explained.

'Dan said the plural of 'dominus' was 'dominoes,' and when Miss Blake said it wasn't he said he supposed it was 'backgammon,' and so he had to write it out twice – for cheek, you know.'

It was a public teasing of John. Miss Blaikie, who was taken on in May 1903 for £60 a year as the new governess, was always keeping him in when Elsie was allowed out to play. John's work, both here in this room and later when he went away to school, was never up to scratch. Kipling often wrote to him with a characteristic mixture of reproach and affection:

Dear old man,
Life's a damn interesting thing, my son, and I want you to have a good life. But you won't if you don't dig out. I've just met a youth who is a slacker. My gawd, such a slacker. He gave me cold shudders at the thought that you might grow into such another.

A few months later, the rather severe tone was tempered by this: 'I wish I didn't miss you as much as I do, old man. You were a huge nuisance at times but I seem to have got fond of you in some incomprehensible way.'

FURNITURE

An Edwardian red lacquer bureau cabinet. This may well have been bought by the Kiplings when they were refurnishing the room for Elsie.

The other furniture is English, 17th-century.

PICTURES

Five sepia watercolours by John Lockwood Kipling, depicting various Indian trades and professions.

A framed map of Sussex.

SCULPTURE

P. LYNGE-HUTCHINSON
Rudyard Kipling (1865–1936)
Bronze bust
Begun towards the end of Kipling's life and completed posthumously.

TEXTILES

LEFT OF FIREPLACE AND OVER DOOR:

Two samplers, which were part of a collection that belonged to the Kiplings.

CERAMICS

IN UPPER PART OF LACQUER CABINET:

A 19th-century porcelain dessert service painted with botanical specimens and a pair of Staffordshire pottery groups. Neither belonged to Kipling.

ON CHIMNEYPIECE:

A group of early 19th-century Chinese Nanking blue-and-white porcelain. It is part of a large collection of varying dates that the Kiplings used for decoration here and in the Dining Room.

CHAPTER TWO
THE GARDEN AND MILL

Our England is a garden, and such gardens are not made
By Singing:– 'Oh, how beautiful' and sitting in the
shade,
While better men than we go out and start their working
lives
At grubbing weeds from gravel paths with broken dinner-
knives.

'The Glory of the Garden'

THE QUARTER DECK

Outside Elsie Kipling's Sitting Room, a door leads to the south-west front of the house and the Quarter Deck. This broad flagged terrace extends to the western border of the garden and is raised above the level of the main lawn, which is prone to flooding by the River Dudwell. Over the Parlour window on the west front is a trumpet creeper (*Campsis grandiflora*), whose tubular orange flowers appear in the late summer. The spring borders were designed by Graham Stuart Thomas, the National Trust's former Gardens Adviser.

THE POND AND ROSE GARDEN

'The house stands like a beautiful cup on a saucer to match,' as a member of Kipling's family described it. Nathaniel Lloyd, the great expert on English furniture and brickwork, writing in 1919, emphasised how the garden relies on discretion and restraint for its effects:

There is nothing fussy, nothing showy, nothing savouring of the villa, not even a flower bed. There is none of the shopkeeper's desire to dress the front as if it were a shop window. All here is reticent.

The Kiplings undoubtedly believed in that aesthetic, but the garden was also for fun, particularly the

(Right) Kipling's 1906 design for the Rose Garden

pond, which was given a shallow concrete bottom so that it did not matter if children, or anyone else, fell in. Here the nervous young American Arthur Gordon is put at his ease. Kipling greeted him for the first time in his life with the words:

'I was just going to inspect my navy.' He led me speechless to a pond at the end of the garden and there was the navy: a 6-foot skiff with hand-cranked paddle-wheels. 'You can be the engine-room,' he said. 'I'll be the passenger-list.'

I was so agitated that I cranked too hard. The

Bateman's from the south-west; watercolour by
E. J. Poynter, 1913 (Hall)

paddle-wheel broke and there I was marooned in the middle of a fishpond with Rudyard Kipling. He began to laugh, and so did I, and the ice was broken.

Next to the names of those who had fallen in, he made a small note in the Visitors' Book: 'FIP' ['Fell in Pond'].

The avenue of pleached limes had been planted in 1898, before Kipling arrived, but the pond, the Rose Garden at the far end, and the encircling yew hedges were all laid out according to his own design, which still hangs in the Study. The garden was paid for out of the £7,700 he received for the Nobel Prize in 1907. The previous year, on 3 August 1906, a frustratingly short note appears in the Visitors' Book: 'To lunch Mr Robinson. Suggests alterations in garden.' Was this William Robinson of Gravetye Manor, the great Edwardian garden designer and writer?

The semicircular wooden seat backed by a yew hedge was a garden feature that seems to have been invented by the Arts and Crafts architect Walter Godfrey. Mirroring it at the opposite end of the pond is another yew alcove containing a sundial inscribed 'It is later than you think'. William Ramsey, a neighbour, was taken by Kipling to be shown it one afternoon. Ramsey couldn't quite work out why Kipling had done this until Carrie said off-handedly: 'Oh, Rud always brings his guests to read that when he thinks they should be going home.' The Rose Garden is planted with 'Betty Prior', 'Mrs Inge Paulson' and 'Frensham' in shades of pink and red, underplanted with spring-flowering narcissi and *Muscari* in yellow and blue.

THE WILD GARDEN AND RIVER DUDWELL

Beyond the hedge, the formality of the garden loosens, and a half-wild garden spreads along the banks of the River Dudwell. Trees and flowering shrubs are planted in rough grass, which in spring is

The Wild Garden

carpeted with daffodils, scillas, wood anemones and fritillaries. Kipling always kept a well-thumbed copy of C. A. Johns's *Flowers of the Field* by him. Introductions along the river bank include the April-flowering hardy yellow Arum lily, *Lysichiton americanus*, and the Brazilian gunnera, a very Kiplingesque plant, with its huge jungle-like leaves. Over them grow a Turkey oak, a silver weeping lime and a smoke tree. Above the second bridge leading to Park Mill is a 'wriggly' nut tree, *Corylus avellana* 'Contorta'.

Here, during and after the Great War, Kipling brought the Irish Guards officers he was interviewing for his book, giving them an afternoon's fishing for brown trout. 'It's a strange thing,' Kipling told his secretary Dorothy Ponton, 'these war-worn youngsters, who didn't mind killing Huns, will blanch and squirm when the moment arrives to attach a worm to the end of the hook. "Please would you mind doing it?" they will plead and look the other way.'

Before the cataclysm, the river at the bottom of the garden had been the access to hidden and unimagined worlds. The deep, alluring bed of the Dudwell opens the Puck story called 'The Knights of the Joyous Venture':

It was too hot to run about in the open, so Dan asked their friend, old Hobden, to take their own dinghy from the pond and put her on the brook at the bottom of the garden. Her painted name was the *Daisy*, but for exploring expeditions she was the *Golden Hind* or the *Long Serpent*, or some such suitable name. Dan hiked and howked with a boat-hook (the brook was too narrow for sculls), and Una punted with a piece of hop-pole. When they came to a very shallow place (the *Golden Hind* drew quite three inches of water) they disembarked and scuffled her over the gravel by her tow-rope, and when they reached the overgrown banks beyond the garden they pulled themselves upstream by the low branches. . . .

Even on the shaded water the air was hot and heavy with drowsy scents, while outside, through breaks in the trees, the sunshine burned the pasture like fire.

THE MILL

The longer he was at Bateman's, the older Kipling made his treasured Park Mill. The present building was put up in about 1750. There are documents showing that two mills were built, by royal command, in Burwash parish in 1246–8, but Kipling claimed in December 1902 that he then owned 'an old house and a mill (water) that dates from 1196'. No one knows where he got that date from, but by 1907 he was saying that the Mill 'knew Domesday Book backwards and forwards' and that the noise of its revolving wheels said as much: 'Book – Book – Domesday Book'.

In the later Puck stories, the mill, he came to think, had been there since Roman times and was part of the ancient mythologised landscape that Kipling made of the Dudwell valley:

A rainy afternoon drove Dan and Una over to play pirates in the Little Mill. If you don't mind rats on the rafters and oats in your shoes, the mill-attic with its trap-doors and inscriptions on beams about floods and sweethearts, is a splendid place. It is lighted by a foot-square window, called Duck Window, that looks across to Little Lindens [Rye Green] farm, and the spot where Jack Cade [leader of the Kentish rebellion in 1450] was killed.

Despite its antiquity, Kipling showed it little respect. Within weeks of arrival he de-clutched the 18th-century corn-grinding mechanism and installed a water turbine made by Gilbert Gilkes & Co. in the mill dam. It drove a generator designed by Christy Bros. and Middleton, Electrical Engineers, of Chelmsford, which, by a 250-yard length of buried deep-sea cable, led to storage batteries in a Bateman's outhouse. They supplied enough current to light ten 60-watt bulbs in the house for about four hours every evening and needed the generator to

The Mill

*The first floor
of the Mill*

run for about three hours a day to charge them up. His adviser was Sir William Willcocks, a classic imperial figure, who, in a clash of scales that Kipling enjoyed, had previously installed the first Aswan Dam ('a trifling affair on the Nile') and, as he wrote to John, had 'wandered through Babylon and Baghdad making dams on the Tigris and Euphrates. One of the most interesting chaps I have ever met.'

In 1968–75 the building, which had fallen into a sad state of disrepair, was restored. The Royal Engineers rebuilt the turbine-generator, and a team of volunteers laid a new ground floor, repaired the timber framework for the machinery, overhauled the wooden wheels and cogs, and fitted a new waterwheel.

On entering the mill, go straight up the stairway on the left to the first floor, called the 'stone floor'.

FIRST FLOOR

Corn is fed by the miller from bins in the attic into the hopper, and from there down into the wooden casing, in which it is ground between the upper, revolving 'running' stone and the stationary 'bed' stone. Another pair of millstones on this floor has been exposed to show the grooving on their working faces. The yellow-painted machine nearby was used for winnowing corn, that is, separating the chaff from the grain.

Leave the first floor by the other stairway.

GROUND FLOOR

Here you can see the various toothed cogs which translate the slow, vertical motion of the water-wheel (linked to the 'great spur wheel' at the bottom) into the faster, horizontal action of the millstones on the floor above. From a position near the rear door, the miller can adjust the gap between the stones and so the grade of flour produced.

PARK MILL COTTAGE

The chauffeur lived in the cottage attached to the mill itself. In the new Park Mill Cottage next to it (which was converted from an oast-house by the Kiplings), the secretary, the governess and their own maid all lived, listening to 'the quiet chug-chug of the dynamo', as the waters of the Dudwell ran slowly through the turbine.

Retracing your steps to the formal garden and leaving the house on the right, you come to the oast-houses (now the National Trust shop), one of which supports a dovecote put up in the late 19th century. Beyond are the potting sheds and the garage which now houses Kipling's Rolls-Royce.

THE ROLLS-ROYCE

Kipling was one of those pioneer motorists for whom a short drive in a 'horseless carriage' was an adventure, every policeman a natural enemy, and a return to base in the same day cause for thanksgiving. Kipling's first 'very own' motor, a temperamental steam-car, frequently drove him to despair.

'Amelia' was the first of several early Lanchesters to occupy the Bateman's garage. Number sixteen off the production line, she was a two-cylinder 10 horsepower model with tiller-steering and perfect springing, but of a fickle disposition. Her designer, F. W. Lanchester, became a frequent visitor in response to urgent telegrams. 'Amelia' was the original of the big black-dashed 'Octopod' that 'sang like a six-inch shell' across the Sussex Downs in *Steam Tactics*, the first of many farcical motoring tales that helped to defray her, and her successors', repair costs.

In 1911 Kipling acquired his first Rolls-Royce. He bought the car shown here, a Phantom I 40–50 horsepower model, in 1928 for £2,833 18s 6d. (It is on permanent loan to the Trust from Sir Jack Hayward.) 'It is the only car I can afford,' he said of a machine that was built to last – and to appreciate in value. He ran it until 1932, when he bought another, which was his final car.

Kipling kept diaries of his regular motor tours at home and abroad – from laconic reports of mileages and hotels to vivid, pages-long accounts of the day's events. 'Even R-R's not perfect', he noted as the 'Duchess' listed drunkenly with a broken spring on the war-torn French roads. To Kipling the motor car was a time-machine in which centuries slid by like milestones, revealing 'a land of stupefying marvels and mysteries. . . . A day in the car in an English county is a day in some fairy museum where all the exhibits are alive and real.'

The ground floor of the Mill

CHAPTER THREE
KIPLING AND BATEMAN'S

'England is a wonderful land,' Kipling wrote in 1902, announcing his arrival at Bateman's to his life-long friend, the Harvard critic Charles Eliot Norton, 'It is the most marvellous of all foreign countries I have ever been in. It is made up of trees and green fields and mud and the gentry. and at last I'm one of the gentry.'

Of course he wasn't. Few aspects of England were more anathema to him than the county set, and he spent half a lifetime steering away from it. 'Josephine, after considering things in her little head, has pronounced that "this England is stuffy",' he had reported on 1896. It was the word Kipling himself chose to use, writing to Rhodes in South Africa: 'England is a stuffy little place, mentally, morally and physically.' To another correspondent he went on:

I have been studying my fellow-countrymen from the outside. We are a rummy breed – and O Lord the ponderous wealthy society. Torquay is such a place as I do desire to upset by dancing through it with nothing on but my spectacles. Villas, clipped hedges and shaven lawns; fat old ladies with respirators and obese landaus. The Almighty is a discursive and frivolous trifler compared with some of them.

But the land is undeniably lovely.

England was beautiful, but it was wasted on the English – or at least that section of them who claimed to own the place.

Why then did Kipling come to live among them, in a dark house, in a damp valley, surrounded by the small 'c' conservatism with which he was so impatient and by which he felt so stifled, when he had spent most of his youth in India and the United States, and could have lived almost anywhere he chose?

Apart from everything else, England was so small. If there is one quality which can encompass Kipling's character and work, it is an openness to the variety of life and experience, an eager absorption of the world's phenomena, all the way from machinery to metaphysics, from the concrete substance of actual things to their deep historical and spiritual implications. There was what Angus Wilson called simply 'a largeness to Kipling's spirit', and England seemed, at least to begin with, to lack that largeness. That scale of existence belonged to the imperial life and the vast landscapes on which the dramas of empire were enacted. They were a reproach to the small scale of England, its petty, closed, stale restrictedness, its pale sunshine and its anaemic breezes. In one of his great cockney-imperial poems, 'Chant-Pagan', written just as he was arriving at Bateman's, he puts the question into the mouth of a discharged English irregular, a man who has 'watched 'arf a world/'Eave up all shiny with dew':

'Ow can I ever take on
With awful old England again,
An' 'ouses both sides of the street,
An' 'edges two sides of the lane,
An' the parson an' gentry between,
An' touchin' my 'at when we meet –
   Me that 'ave been what I've been?

The answer lay in the appeal of history. If England lacked the sheer extent of empire, it more than made up for it in the depth of its history. At Bateman's, Kipling's mind moved from the epic and present extent of the Indian and African landscapes to the more ambiguous presence of the past as he found it everywhere in the Sussex Weald around him. In many forms, in stories both for children and for adults and in poetry, the house and the landscape of the Dudwell valley came to shape the second half of his life's work. 'Kipling knew something of the things which are underneath,' T. S. Eliot said of him, 'and of the things which are beyond the frontier.' This valley introduced him to 'the things that were underneath'. As he was to write almost at the end of

Rudyard Kipling, painted by John Collier in 1900, two years before he bought Bateman's (Staircase)

his life, with an air of amazement and gratitude at what this landscape had given him:

The Old Things of our valley glided into every aspect of our outdoor works. Earth, Air, Water and People had been – I saw it at last – in full conspiracy to give me ten times as much as I could compass, even if I wrote a complete history of England, as much as that might have touched or reached our valley.

It was, as Eliot later said, 'a deepening of the imperial into the historical imagination'. The Dudwell valley, with the richness of its history to hand, its air of magic, its soil and woods thick with meanings that survive in fragments, parts of a larger whole lurking just beneath the surface, became Kipling's province, an empire of the imagination. The scale was here, if only you knew how to look for it, to read the signs the place was giving you.

From the outside, the Kiplings' Bateman's looked conventional enough. There was quite a staff, housed in the various buildings scattered around the estate. There were five maids in 1910: Georgine, Ada, Ellen, Long Nellie and Elsie Martin. Both Elsie Martin's parents also worked for the Kiplings, there was a Hobbs and a Drowbridge, and a Moore, who looked after the car. A governess and a secretary and a stream of much-loved rather wayward Aberdeen

The Hall, where the Kiplings' visitors were given tea

terriers completed the ménage. At various times, between sixteen and twenty people lived full-time at Bateman's.

A large number of visitors came both to stay and for either lunch or tea. It was a constantly, if never hectically, social place, and the Visitors' Book, kept by Kipling rather than signed by the guests, articulates at least the surface of life here. One or other member of the extended family is almost always there: the Baldwins, Lady Burne-Jones, various Macdonald cousins, Kipling's sister Trix Fleming and several Poynter cousins and nephews and nieces parade through its pages. Men on business – H. A. Gwynne, a leading journalist and in the early years of the century an advocate of Kipling's conservative agenda; A. P. Watt, Kipling's literary agent and stalwart ally for 40 years; Frank Doubleday, his American publisher; Max Aitken, the Canadian journalist later to become Lord Beaverbrook – all come, sometimes to stay, more often for lunch. Figures from the empire, Rhodesia, the Malay States, the Dominion of Canada, arrive bringing news, seeking advice. A very few literary figures appear: Henry James once or twice, who had admired Kipling when young but disliked Carrie ('a hard, devoted, capable little person'), and Rider Haggard much more often. Henry Pegram, the sculptor, comes to stay for four nights from 3 to 7 August 1907, to sculpt Elsie's profile. Those who come by motor, as Kipling meticulously notes, are more often than not late and so miss lunch.

The flow remains unstaunched almost until the end. In 1933, for example, the Kiplings, both chronically ill, he with duodenal ulcers, she with agonising back pain and rheumatism, nevertheless had 140 people to lunch or tea here, including T. E. Lawrence on 14 July, a man Kipling had once admired but came to distrust as a showman and a charlatan. Such sociability throws into a different light the received idea of their rigid reclusiveness. They disliked the vulgarly intrusive press (but had many journalist friends), the boringly middle-aged, the county set, but they liked the interestingly old, the young almost without reserve and the family, in all its cousinly ramifications. The final entry is on 4–6 January 1936, three days before Kipling signs

Bateman's from Donkey Hill

his will, twelve days before he dies of peritonitis after his gastric ulcer haemorrhaged in London. After the words 'Mr and Mrs Mike Mason', entered for those dates, Carrie writes '*The End*' and underlines it.

Thirty-four years earlier, the Kiplings had arrived at Bateman's bursting with energy and zest. Ambrose Poynter, Rudyard's architect cousin, was brought in to supervise the improvements: the new panelling, the new storm door for the kitchen, the partition for the pantry, the new electricity supply, the conversion of the oast-houses for a gardener's and then servants' accommodation, the limewashing of the entire top floor – in all a hurricane of activity in the autumn and winter of 1902.

The house had come with only 33 acres of ground immediately around it but the Kiplings set about enlarging the estate, spreading out east and west along the valley and up to the main road on the ridge above them: Rye Green Farm and 51 acres in November 1903, another sixteen acres at Little

Bateman's and Upper and Lower Oxfield the following September, Dudwell Mill and farm with extra land in February 1905, brickworks and more land west of Bell Alley Lane the following January, followed by Fenners Farm in September 1912. The process went on in scraps and patches right up until 1928. By the end, through fourteen separate conveyances, they had assembled about 300 acres, pretty much the restoration of the historic Bateman's estate, with some more on the side.

This was deeply committed acquisitiveness. There was certainly no need involved. By the Thirties Kipling was earning more than £32,000 a year from his writing (even if £17,000 of that was going in tax), and there was no thought of making a living out of the land. Acquisition, the creation of a protective buffer around the house itself, was the sole cause. It found its equivalent, inside the house, in the scores of tiny objects gathered in every cupboard and on most shelves, so that at times Bateman's today can still seem like a cabinet of talismans, a house filled with fragments shored against their ruin.

There is a moment in one of Kipling's most apparently autobiographical of Sussex stories, 'An Habitation Enforced', first published in 1909, which dramatises this magic in the acquisition of place. An American couple come to England, for the balm and cure of the landscape, the husband having suffered a nervous breakdown through overwork. They fall in love with a house called Friars Pardon, which, after weeks of walking and waiting and watching, they finally decide to buy. One day the husband announces to his wife the successful conclusion of the deal. It is a critical moment in Kipling's English fiction, the incantation of places bought and owned:

'Friars Pardon – Friars Pardon!' Sophie chanted rapturously, her dark gray eyes big with delight. 'All the farms? Gale Anstey, Burnt House, Rocketts, the Home Farm, and Griffons? Sure you've got 'em all?'
  'Sure.' He smiled.
  'And the woods? High Pardons Wood, Lower Pardons, Suttons, Dutton's Shaw, Reuben's Ghyll, Maxey's Ghyll, and both the Oak Hangers? Sure you've got 'em all?'
  'Every last stick. . . .'

Burnt House is the name of a farm within a mile of Bateman's; Gale Anstey recalls the name of a much-loved Baldwin house at Astley in Worcestershire; the naming of small woods as Shaws and of sharply wooded dells as Ghylls are both habits of the Sussex Weald. There can be little doubt that this is a straightforward transcription of life into work, of place as cure.

  Later in the story, Sophie, who is in effect a deeply loving portrayal by Kipling of a wife he knew the rest of the world largely disliked, learns that she is pregnant. Anything to do with children is highly charged for Kipling, and this is a signal for a second strongly explicit moment in which Kipling portrays the house as an ally and protector, guaranteeing a continuation of the line:

Of a sudden the house she had bought for a whim stood up as she had never seen it before, low-fronted, broad-winged, ample, prepared by course of generations for all such things. As it had steadied her when it lay desolate, so now that it had meaning from their few months of life within, it soothed and promised good. She went alone and quickly into the hall, and

kissed either door-post, whispering 'Be good to me. *You* know! You've never failed in your duty yet.'

If this is veering into the sentimental, implying a lack of artistic control, that can only be because Kipling was describing an emotional reality in his own life. In the concluding poem, in which 'the land of their fathers' speaks to the 'children' who have returned to it, the meaning could not be made more clear:

Over their heads in the branches
  Of their new-bought, ancient trees,
I weave an incantation,
  And draw them to my knees.

Scent of smoke in the evening,
  Smell of rain in the night,
The hours, the days and the seasons
  Order their souls aright;

The place – 'new-bought, ancient' concentrates their position at Bateman's as succinctly as one could – is a cure for sorrows and unrootedness.

  Both Kiplings took a real and detailed interest in the affairs of the land they acquired. Much of it was tenanted, and Kipling came to loathe and distrust the short-sightedness, as he saw it, of tenant farmers, driving the land as hard as they could for immediate profit, with no thought to the future. These, of course, were the days before legislation had guaranteed farming tenants and their families security of tenure over several generations. It was also a period of acute agricultural depression, in which cheap, imported grain and meat from the New World were driving swathes of European farmers out of business. It is not surprising that the Burwash farmers were not keeping their properties in the most pristine condition.

  Kipling showed little tolerance of this. He was working to a different agenda, a vision of an historical landscape on which such modern failings were little more than excrescences. There had been a modern, intensive chicken plant within a couple of miles of Bateman's since the 1880s, there had been savagely suppressed riots by agricultural labourers in Burwash and the surrounding district in the 1830s, but you would never guess it from anything Kipling wrote about his Sussex world. He was not, of course, unaware of the changes occurring in rural

England, and a late story like 'The Wish House' draws its energy from those changes, but the imaginative look, the source of meaning, is backwards, into time and the continuities that survive, even if in half-forgotten fragments.

As soon as he could, Kipling took the farms back in hand and managed them directly. Rider Haggard, conducting a long campaign for the regeneration of English agriculture, advised him at every turn. Writing to Haggard in 1925, Kipling adopted the tone of the weary old landowner gamely struggling with the intractability of land and men:

Dear old man,

Now hear me moan! The land is porridge. We send out whiskey, with the drenches, to the wretched little calves that are now being born; we litter down twice a day and the wet bog swallows it all: *all* my winter wheat is dead. No one has been able to set foot on the land since November and *all* my sheep have foot rot, so we are mending roads out of a newly opened quarry (did I tell you) and the men are so bored with past idleness that they are working with interest! Call me a liar, but it's true!

One can tell that in part at least it is all something of a game, and of course the farms provided endless opportunities for the ever-buoyant playful impishness which every visitor to Bateman's always remarked on. There was a dairy herd of Guernsey cows, which as Dorothy Ponton, the Kiplings' secretary, coolly noted, always cost more to feed than their produce was worth. But they were there, as so much else on the estate, largely for aesthetic reasons. A dairy herd looks and smells nice, the cattle suit the landscape, the calves can be given charming names (which they were by Kipling himself): Bateman's Baby, Bateman's Blizzard, Bateman's Bunting and Bateman's Butterpat all grew up here in the early years of the century and went on, to their proprietor's unconcealed delight, to win prizes at the Tunbridge Wells cattle show. Later a herd of the beautiful conker-red Sussex beef cattle was added, again largely for looks, for a sense of completeness. There were bees and geese, which turned in a handsome profit, and chickens that provided the occasion for a classic Kipling piece of 'take nothing for granted if you can check it'. One

Kipling being paddled across the Bateman's pond

Boxing Day, he and Sir John Bland-Sutton, the President of the Royal College of Surgeons, who for years struggled ineffectually to cure Kipling's stomach pains, claimed one could hear a chicken's gizzard clicking. Kipling insisted it should be checked. In *Something of Myself*, he makes it seem as if he is the unwilling partner in the escapade:

We caught an outraged pullet. John soothed her for a while (he said her pulse was a hundred and twenty-six), and held her to his ear, 'She clicks all right,' he announced. 'Listen.' I did, and there was click enough for a lecture. '*Now* we can go back to the house,' I pleaded. 'Wait a bit. Let's catch that cock. He'll click better.' We caught him after a loud and long chase, and he clicked like a solitaire board.

There were pigs as well – far too expensive when bought, as he complained to his son John away at school in 1908: 'By the way yesterday the new pigs came – they are both black and they are the smallest we've ever had. They cost eleven bob each and I assure you, Sir, they don't look much bigger than kittens.' His cousin Stanley Baldwin was another serious porcophile, and at Christmas 1919 Kipling gave him a small wooden pig with the following verses inscribed on its flank:

Some to Women, some to Wine –
Some to Wealth or Power incline –
Proper people cherish Swine.
Cattle from the Argentine –
Poultry tough as office twine –
Give no pleasure when we dine.
But, from nose-tip unto chine,
Via every *intestine*,
Nothing is amiss in Swine.
Roast or smoked or soaked in brine –
(We have proved it, Cousin mine)
Every part of him is fine.
So, till Income Tax decline,
Or Truth exist across the Rhine,
Or [Lloyd] George can speak it, praise we Swine,
Common, honest, decent Swine.

These moments of hilarity were of course only part of the man. Throughout his life, Kipling veered between them and bouts of acute depression. Angus Wilson called him 'a gentle-violent man, holding his despairs in with an almost superhuman stoicism'. Only with the resolute support of Carrie, managing

him, organising him and protecting him, was Kipling able to maintain the equilibrium that allowed him to work. Bateman's, and the estate they assembled around it, was an essential tool in that process. It was down in the valley, away from the road, away from the village, surrounded by hedges and high walls. Even though they knew it to be rather gloomy, already with the air of sadness it still has in its rooms even on a sunny day, it has the look of a haven about it, almost a fortress, stony-faced, protective. It was a place where they could pull up a metaphorical drawbridge behind them.

There was more to it than simple anti-sociability. A passage from *Something of Myself* provides the key. Kipling is describing his own magical practices as a boy:

When my father sent me a *Robinson Crusoe*, . . . I set up in business alone as a trader with savages . . . in a mildewy basement room. . . . My apparatus was a coconut shell strung on a red cord, a tin trunk, and a piece of packing case which kept off any other world. . . . If the bit of board fell, I had to begin the magic all over again. I have learned since from children who play much alone that this rule of 'beginning again in a pretended game' is not uncommon. The magic, you see, lies in a ring or fence that you take refuge in.

The last sentence could be a description of Bateman's itself and of the place of the Dudwell valley in Kipling's later years. It is the magical zone into which others do not intrude and whose power and secret relies on a vigilant patrolling of the boundaries. Carrie was the Keeper of the Gate and there is a story remembered in Burwash from the Kiplings' later years which dramatises this in an extraordinary and otherworldly way.

One of the Bateman's calves was to be slaughtered for its thymus gland, which is at its largest in young animals and still thought by some to contain life-enhancing juices. After John Kipling went missing at the Battle of Loos in 1915, his father suffered repeated and acute gastric pain. The calf's thymus may have been intended to alleviate this. After the gland had been extracted from the animal, Carrie insisted that the rest of the carcass should not be used for meat. It was to be buried, not on the farm but inside the garden, and the ground over it raked to a fine tilth which would show any disturbance. After that tilth had been prepared, she signed the raked ground with her own name.

This is an odd and disturbing image: the life-giving calf, dead and signed for in the garden, locked away from the rest of the world by a mother who had seen the death of two of her three children and shown no public pain. It seems like an unconsciously magical and demonic act, a sacrifice in a Sussex garden, a thousand miles from the world of Burwash and the straightforward use of animals for meat, but rather near to the world of Kipling's own poetry and its sense of the enigmatic undercurrents flowing everywhere beneath the surface of the ordinary. It is a symptom of the tension under which they were both living, remembered, perhaps a little unfairly, by their daughter Elsie after they had died:

Carrie Kipling; by Philip Burne-Jones, 1899 (Study)

My mother introduced into everything she did, and even permeated the life of her family with, a sense of strain and worry amounting sometimes to hysteria. Her possessive and rather jealous nature, both with regard to my father and to us children, made our lives very difficult, while her uncertain moods kept us apprehensively on the alert for possible storms.

There can be no doubt that Carrie's protectiveness was, in a way, obsessive. In the later years she would not let a single piece of Kipling's handwriting leave the house; everything he wrote had to be typed out by the secretary. When she found the manuscript of *The Irish Guards in the Great War* about to be sent to the publisher with some last-minute handwritten alterations by the author, she insisted that the entire text be re-typed. Kipling himself had to apologise to the secretary.

There can be no doubt, on the other side, that his wife's role as his guard dog enabled him to pursue a complex and disturbing imaginative life with extraordinary persistence and in the face of great sorrow over the death of two of his children, enormous suffering from his undiagnosed ulcers and their unsatisfactory treatment, and, from the First World War onwards, almost total critical disdain.

Carrie's ferocity allowed Kipling, among many other things, to explore, in private and in all its ramifications, the place where they lived. The landscape and those whom he saw, perhaps a little artificially, bound to it and emanating from it, become the heroes of many of the stories Kipling wrote at Bateman's. The figure of Hobden, the hedger and ditcher, the archetypal Sussex man, whose ancestors had been there for ever, and who knew everything there was to know about the place, appears in story after story and poem after poem. He is Sussex made flesh. Kipling may claim to be the proprietor of a wide stretch of the Dudwell valley, he may hold the deeds, but Hobden *possesses* it:

I have rights of chase and warren as my dignity
    requires,
I can fish – but Hobden tickles. I can shoot – but
    Hobden wires. . . .
Shall I summons him to judgement? I would sooner
    summons Pan.

41

The River Dudwell

Kipling and the Dudwell valley become each other's. He puts his mark on it, in field after field, at the corners of woods and the twisting of the river itself, at farms and at cottages now already in ruins and mossed over. In return, the valley shaped his imagination.

The result now is that if you take a walk along the paths that follow the Dudwell upstream from Bateman's you will find a double history: first the history of the place itself, of the shaping of the valley for ironworking and agriculture, the cutting of the mill leat that runs straight alongside the twisting river, the weirs and sluices for the control of that water, and, above them all, the coppiced woodland that provided the fuel for the furnaces. Overlying that first history, feeding off it, dramatising and enriching it, is the second layer of a writer who came here in early middle age, looking for a sanctuary at a particularly fragile moment in his life and finding it in the consolation and continuities of history. In the stories that Kipling wrote for his children collected as *Puck of Pook's Hill* (published in 1906) and *Rewards and Fairies* (1910), the fragments of a buried past emerge as burning and magical realities for John and Elsie.

Kipling's descriptions of that landscape – and the words he used to describe his relationship to it were 'wonder and desire' – hold good today. There are still trout in the Dudwell and kingfishers fishing for them. Hobden's cottage and the forge have disappeared, and an alder wood now grows over what must always have been the boggy site of them. But the river itself is just as Dan and Una found it one afternoon in the early years of the century:

They were fishing, a few days later, in a bed of the brook that for centuries had cut deep into the soft valley soil. The trees closing overhead made long tunnels through which the sunshine worked in blobs and patches. Down in the tunnels were bars of sand and gravel, old roots and trunks covered with moss or painted red by the irony water; . . . clumps of fern and thirsty shy flowers who could not live away from moisture and shade.

Still, at 'the sadder darker end' of the wood, further along the valley there is:

an old marlpit full of black water, where weepy, hairy moss hangs round the stumps of the willows and the alders. But the birds come to perch on the dead branches, and Hobden says that the bitter willow-water is a sort of medicine for sick animals.

And one can still find oneself there suddenly surprised by something that is at the same time strange and familiar:

'Hst!' he whispered.

He stood still, for not twenty paces away a magnificent dog-fox sat on his haunches and looked at the children as though he were an old friend of theirs.

For the whole performance, Puck, the little brown pointy-eared earth god, is the master of ceremonies. He acts as the compère, rather smoothly and coolly emerging from the leafy wings, presenting the children with the astonishingly immediate and real past, and then just as deftly slipping back into invisibility. In his hands, the boundaries between the real and the imagined are dissolved, the strange and the alien are slickly wafted into concrete existence and with equal panache swept away. Each story ends with that quiver of closure, and each new one begins with a sudden unapologised appearance of the strange. It is as rich and multi-dimensional a description of the landscape as has ever been made. In part it is a game for Kipling, in the same way he would float paper boats down the little streams that crossed his land when taking visitors for walks, but

THE Charter
of
The River

Know all Men by These Presents that I
The Sieur Rudyard Kipling of Batemans in the County
of Sussex
do grant and confirm and by These Presents have granted and confirmed
To John Kipling and Elsie his Sister [quamdiu se bene gesserint]
The Charter Liberties, Freedoms & Benefits all and singular of
all that portion of the Dudwell River lying and situate between Turbine Point
and the Great Ash commonly called Cape Turnagain for their private and
particular use behoof advantage ownership disport and delight
without let hindrance molestation tax toll due fee or Service Excepting always
such Knightly Love and Fealty as already subsists between Us.
That The Said John Kipling and Elsie his sister shall be at all times
free to come and go and look and Know — whether shod or barefoot —
between the two points aforesaid and to name and claim and use for
a game all Bays Points, Bars, Capes, Promontories, Shingles, Shallows
Deeps, Ditches, Drains, Pools and Trees as best shall them please.
And Furthermore by Virtue of These Presents they shall freely enjoy
and exercise The High The Low and The Middle Justice upon and over
all Birds, Beasts, Reptiles, Fishes and Insects as may by custom inhabit
or by accident enter the aforesaid Domain whereof the Two aforesaid —
to wit John Kipling and Elsie his Sister—stand accountable and whereof
they are sieged and possessed.
And the Said John Kipling and Elsie his sister shall hold and employ and dig and
enjoy for their sole selves without tribute to their liege all Gold, Precious and
Sub-Precious Stones, Metals minerals Mines and Quarries which they may
by art or accident discover within the limits of their Domain aforesaid
And They shall hold further both together and sole All rights of Free Forest
Warren and Chase: Turbary: Common: Loppage and Pannage with all such
other Rights and Prerogatives as do vest in the lawful Possessors of such Domains
according to the Custom and Prescription of Old England
Provided Always that the Said John Kipling and Elsie his Sister shall in nowise wage War overt or
covert against their Liege Lord but shall always with speed and diligence warn him of all
Plots and Discomfitures against him directed and in his cause shall bear him true and
Knightly Service NOR shall they fortify by Arts or defend with Arms and Engines
any Bank, Ford, Passage or Pass or any strong place make or suffer to be made
within the length of their dominion. Nor shall they hold against their Liege Lord or his Peoples
any of his household or people any bridge by which their Liege-Lord and his Peoples
are used and wonted to cross the River aforesaid at any place: nor shall they
mud Earth Grass or leaves or water throw at or against their Liege-Lord or their
Law Mother but shall in always matters and concerns abide Peaceful, Loyal,
orderly and discreet as Faithful lieges.
To The Which Charter I the Sieur Rudyard Kipling
of Batemans in the County of Sussex have set my seal
This Nineteenth Day of June, in the Year of our Lord
one Thousand nine hundred and Six
June: 19: 1906.

The Charter of the River, a mock-medieval document drawn up by Kipling in 1906 assigning the Dudwell to his children 'for their private and particular use, behoof, advantage, ownership, disport and delight'

underlying it is a more serious purpose, an attempt to convey the extra dimension to the place of which he was constantly aware. He put this nearly prosaic, everyday sense of the hauntedness of the landscape into one of his most famous lyrics, 'The Way Through the Woods':

They shut the road through the woods
   Seventy years ago.
Weather and rain have undone it again,
   And now you would never know
There was once a road through the woods
   Before they planted the trees.
It is underneath the coppice and heath,
   And the thin anemones.
   Only the keeper sees
That, where the ring-dove broods,
   And the badgers roll at ease,
There was once a road through the woods.

Yet, if you enter the woods
   Of a summer evening late,
When the night air cools on the trout-ringed pools
   Where the otter whistles his mate,
(They fear not men in the woods
   Because they see so few)
You will hear the beat of a horse's feet
   And the swish of a skirt in the dew,
   Steadily cantering through
The misty solitudes,
   As though they perfectly knew
The old lost road through the woods . . .
But there is no road through the woods!

Despite the earlier loss of Josephine, there is an air of completeness to the years at Bateman's before the First World War, of a sort of happiness achieved. Kipling was working hard, being highly productive, pushing his writing into areas it had never been; the place he was living was beautiful, he loved it, and his children were content. Later, after the war, he told Rider Haggard, whose son had also died young, that 'he was never happier than when he knew his boy was asleep in the next room'.

The war itself smashed all that. The Kiplings had already sunk into a state of acute anxiety even before John went missing at the Battle of Loos in September 1915. The Visitors' Book goes suddenly blank and empty for that summer, and those who did see the Kiplings found them in a terribly reduced condition. Haggard reported:

Neither of them looks so well as they did. . . . Their boy John, who is not yet eighteen, is an officer in the Irish Guards and one can see that they are terrified lest he should be sent to the front and killed, as has happened to nearly all the young men they knew.

Kipling was working that year on 'Mary Postgate', one of his grimmest and most ruthless of stories. In it, the heroine doggedly piles on to a bonfire the childhood possessions of the boy she has looked after, who has just been killed in the war. It is Kipling's grindingly moving epitaph for a son who was still alive at the time he wrote it, but whom he knew would soon be dead. Most of the boy's belongings are already useless or broken:

Journey by journey, . . . she brought down in the towel-covered clothes basket, on the wheelbarrow, thumbed and used Hentys, Marryats, Levers, Stevensons, Baroness Orczys, Garvices, schoolbooks and atlases, unrelated piles of the *Motor Cyclist*, the *Light Car*, and catalogues of Olympia Exhibitions; the remnants of a fleet of sailing ships from nine-penny cutters to a three-guinea yacht; a prep-school dressing gown; bats from three-and-sixpence to twenty-four shillings; cricket and tennis balls; disintegrated steam and clockwork locomotives with their twisted rails; a grey and red tin model of a submarine; a dumb gramophone and cracked records; golf clubs that had to be broken across the knee, like his walking sticks, and an assegai. . . .

and so on and on for twice as long again.

John eventually left for France, and Carrie recorded the last moment she saw him in her diary on 17 August 1915: 'John leaves at noon for Warley [his barracks]. He looks very straight and smart and young and brave as he turns at the top of the stairs to say: "Send my love to Daddo".'

John was killed by a shell on his battalion's first day of action near Loos on 27 September 1915. When Kipling came to sum up that day in *The Irish Guards in the Great War*, this is what he wrote:

Of the officers, 2nd Lieutenant Pakenham-Law had died of wounds; 2nd Lieutenants Clifford and Kipling were missing, Captain and Adjutant the Hon. T. E. Vesey, Captain Wynter, Lieutenant Stevens, and 2nd Lieutenants Sassoon and Grayson were wounded, the last being blown up by a shell. It was a fair average for the day of a debut, and taught them somewhat for their future guidance.

What he did not mention is that he paid a British gardener, employed by the War Graves Commission, to sound the Last Post at the Menin Gate every night in remembrance of John, a form of grieving that continued until 1940, when the Germans overran Ypres:

'Have you news of my boy Jack?'
Not this tide.
'When d'you think that he'll come back?'
Not with this wind blowing, and this tide.

A darkness falls on the last years at Bateman's. The Kiplings visit the war cemeteries in France. 'There has never been anything like this in all history,' he says, 'the embalming of a race.' Carrie's eyesight is failing. She becomes rheumatic and diabetic. When in 1924 Elsie leaves to marry George Bambridge, a brother officer of John's, whom neither of her parents likes, Bateman's seems vast, gloomy and empty. 'A train has to stop at some station or other,' he wrote of old age to a friend. 'I only wish it wasn't such an ugly and lonesome place, don't you?' This battered sadness did not make Kipling a bitter man. His generosity of spirit to children and young people remained undiminished. There is a final glimpse of him recorded by the novelist Hugh Walpole:

He is kindly, genial, ready apparently to be friends with anyone but keeping all the time his own guard. . . . Too much of the abnormal in all of us to play about with it. Hates opening up reserves. . . . Ma Kipling . . . a good strong-minded woman who has played watch-dog to him so long that she knows now just how to save him any kind of disturbance, mental, physical, or spiritual. That's *her* job and she does it superbly. . . .

He really, I think, has no vanity. He's a zealous propagandist who, having discovered that the things for which he must propagand are now all out of fashion, guards them jealously and lovingly in his heart, but won't any more trail them about in public.

He walks about the garden, his eyebrows all that are really visible of him. His body is nothing but his eyes are terrific, lambent, kindly, gentle and exceedingly proud. Good to us all and we are all shadows to him.

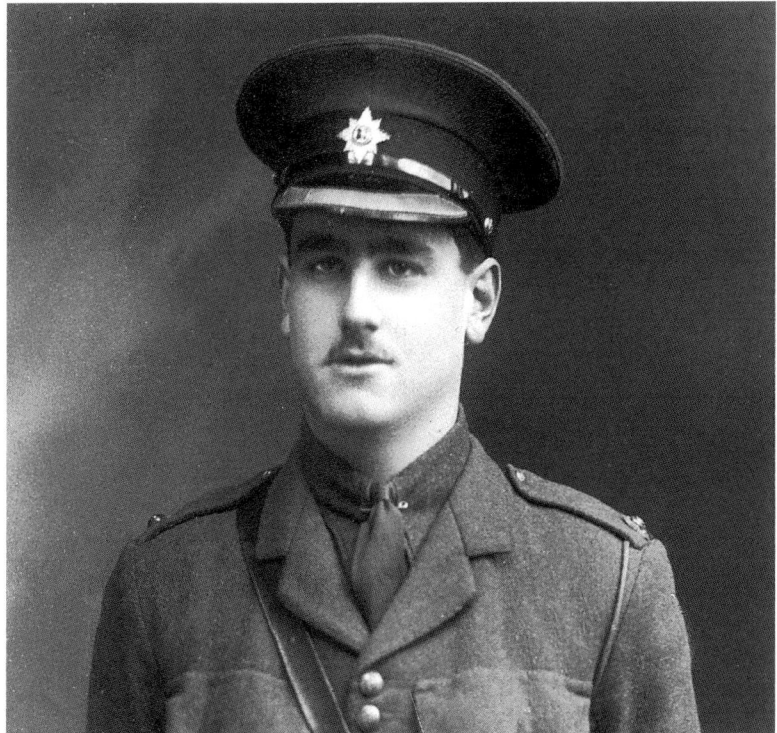

John Kipling in his Irish Guards uniform

FAMILY TREE

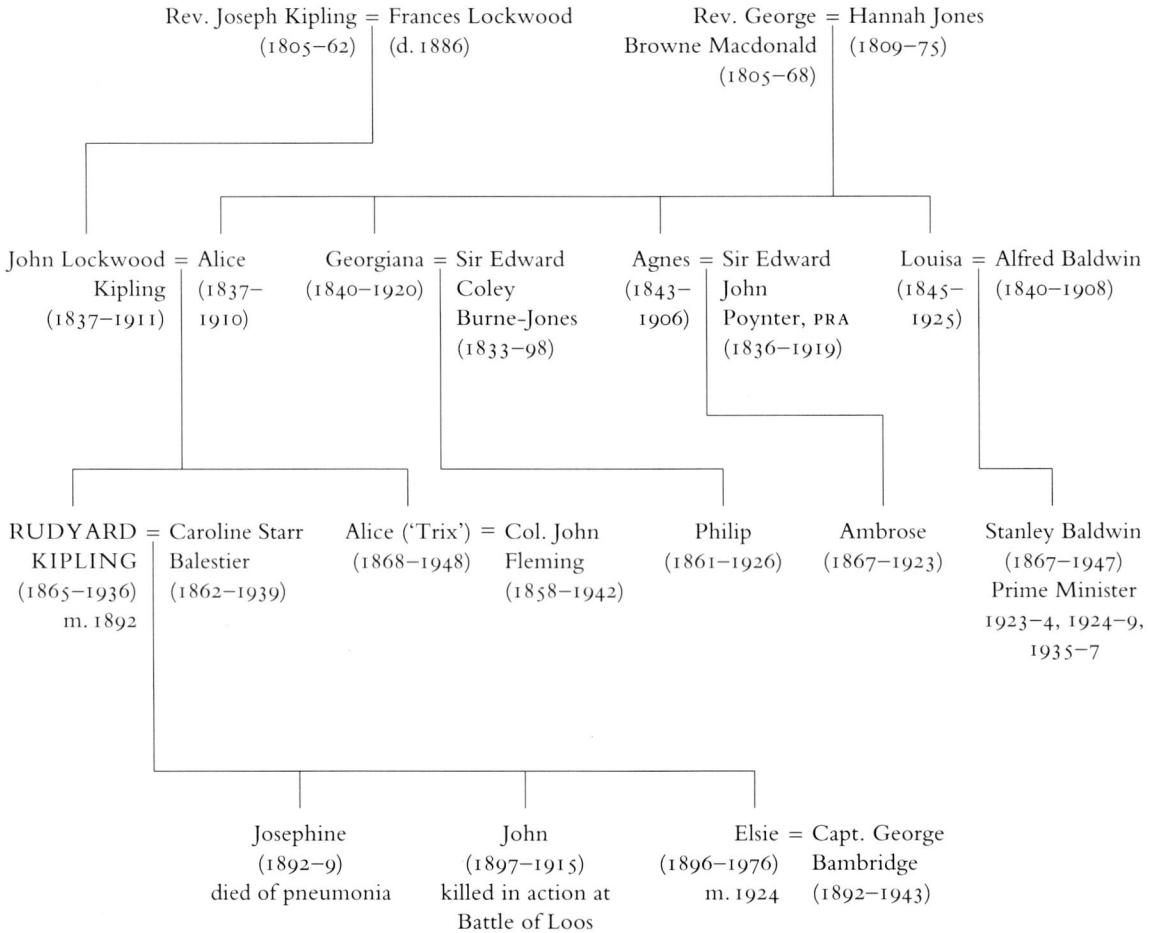

Rev. Joseph Kipling = Frances Lockwood
(1805–62)   (d. 1886)

Rev. George = Hannah Jones
Browne Macdonald   (1809–75)
(1805–68)

John Lockwood = Alice
Kipling   (1837–
(1837–1911)   1910)

Georgiana = Sir Edward
(1840–1920)   Coley
Burne-Jones
(1833–98)

Agnes = Sir Edward
(1843–   John
1906)   Poynter, PRA
(1836–1919)

Louisa = Alfred Baldwin
(1845–   (1840–1908)
1925)

RUDYARD = Caroline Starr
KIPLING   Balestier
(1865–1936)   (1862–1939)
m. 1892

Alice ('Trix') = Col. John
(1868–1948)   Fleming
(1858–1942)

Philip
(1861–1926)

Ambrose
(1867–1923)

Stanley Baldwin
(1867–1947)
Prime Minister
1923–4, 1924–9,
1935–7

Josephine
(1892–9)
died of pneumonia

John
(1897–1915)
killed in action at
Battle of Loos

Elsie = Capt. George
(1896–1976)   Bambridge
m. 1924   (1892–1943)

CHRONOLOGY

CAR-PARK

① 1

② 2

③ 3 ④ 4

⑤ 5

⑥ 6 ⑦ 7

⑧ 8

⑩ 10 ⑨ 9

⑪ 11

⑫ 12

⑬ 13 ⑭ 14

⑮ 15 ⑱ 18

⑯ 16

⑰ 17

⑲ 19

⑳ 20

㉑ 21

㉔ 24

㉒ 22

㉓ 23

N

RIVER
DUDWELL

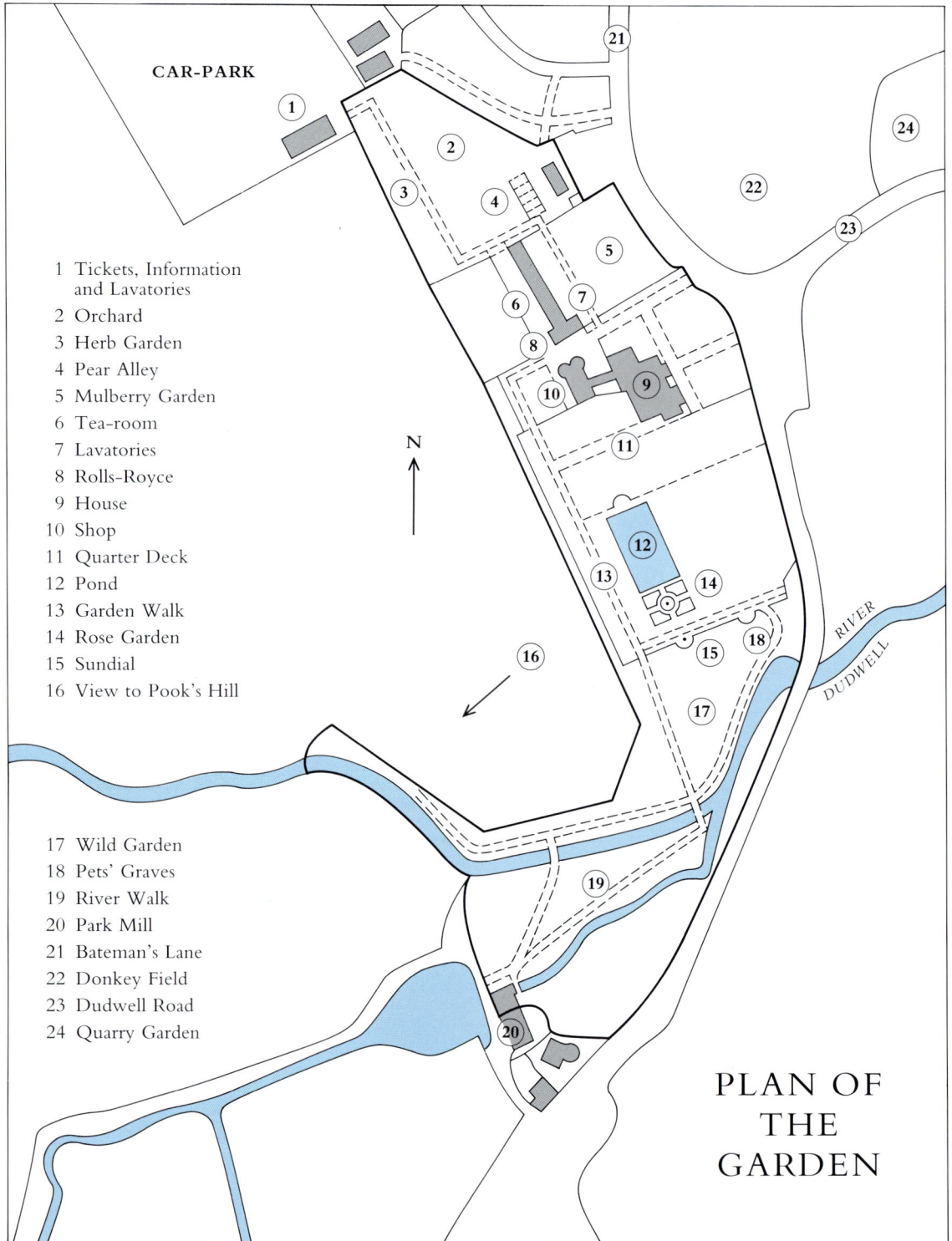

1 Tickets, Information
   and Lavatories
2 Orchard
3 Herb Garden
4 Pear Alley
5 Mulberry Garden
6 Tea-room
7 Lavatories
8 Rolls-Royce
9 House
10 Shop
11 Quarter Deck
12 Pond
13 Garden Walk
14 Rose Garden
15 Sundial
16 View to Pook's Hill

17 Wild Garden
18 Pets' Graves
19 River Walk
20 Park Mill
21 Bateman's Lane
22 Donkey Field
23 Dudwell Road
24 Quarry Garden

PLAN OF
THE
GARDEN